THE *AirForces* BOOK OF THE
F/A-18 HORNET

TIM SENIOR

Above: An F/A-18A from VFA-97 with undercarriage and arrestor hook down and out, captured shortly before landing aboard USS *Kitty Hawk*, underway in the distance. (US Navy)

Key Books Ltd
PO Box 100, Stamford, Lincolnshire, PE9 1XQ, United Kingdom

Telephone: +44 (0) 1780 755131
E-mail: keybooks@keypublishing.com

First published in Great Britain by Key Books Ltd in 2003

ISBN 0-946219-69-9

British Library Cataloguing in Publication Data:
A catalogue record for this book is available from the British Library

Designed by DAG Publications Ltd
Printed in China by Sun Fung Ltd

The author would like to thank Lon O Nordeen and Patricia A Frost at Boeing Military Aircraft, Alan Brown at the NASA Dryden Flight Research Center, and Adrian Urscheler at Swiss Air Force public affairs, together with Jyrki Laukkanen for the Finnish Air Force photographs.

CONTENTS

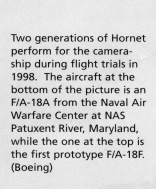

Two generations of Hornet perform for the camera-ship during flight trials in 1998. The aircraft at the bottom of the picture is an F/A-18A from the Naval Air Warfare Center at NAS Patuxent River, Maryland, while the one at the top is the first prototype F/A-18F. (Boeing)

① INTRODUCTION

The development of the F/A-18 Hornet dates back to the late 1960s. Northrop, intent on following up its success with the F-5 family of fighter aircraft, which was then either in production or in the planning stage, revealed a mock-up of the P530 Cobra. Northrop intended to produce this as an air superiority fighter and ground attack aircraft for sale to overseas customers as a replacement for both the F-5 and the Lockheed F-104 Starfighter. The Cobra was designed from the very beginning to be a simple and reliable twin-engine fighter, as well as being easy to maintain and as agile as the F-5 in combat.

With no apparent interest in the project from prospective customers, Northrop revised the design to produce the YF-17, which it subsequently entered into the 1974 Lightweight Fighter (LWF) competition. This would provide the US Air Force with a cheap fighter aircraft to be operated in large numbers alongside the then more expensive McDonnell Douglas F-15 Eagle. The first prototype YF-17 made its maiden flight from Edwards AFB, California, on June 9, 1974, while the second aircraft followed several months later, flying for the first time on August 21. Although both the prototype aircraft performed well, they did suffer some teething problems, as the aircraft were both powered by a pair of the then new and unproven General Electric YJ101 engines.

Although the YF-17 eventually lost the competition to the General Dynamics' YF-16, it did not join the ranks of other prototype fighter aircraft that were simply pushed

to one side and forgotten. Politicians directed the US Navy to integrate technology from both the LWF candidates into a lightweight fighter known as the Naval Air Combat Fighter (NACF) that the US Navy planned to purchase. The requirement called for an aircraft that would replace both the McDonnell F-4 Phantom II in the fighter-bomber role and the LTV A-7 Corsair II in the strike/attack role.

The NACF programme came about as a result of the US Congress cancelling the Lightweight Multi-mission

Right: The YF-17 resulted from Northrop's attempt to continue its success in the lightweight fighter market. The company had already designed and produced the multi-role F-5 Freedom Fighter and the T-38 Talon trainer, both in full production and with healthy order books. Initial designs by Northrop were for a slightly larger multi-role aircraft, which became the P-530 Cobra. When the competition to find a lightweight fighter emerged, Northrop refined the design, initially giving it the P600 designation and this eventually became the YF-17. After the first prototype was rolled out at Northrop's factory at Hawthorne, California, on April 9, 1974, it was transferred to Edwards AFB by road to begin its flight test programme. (Northrop)

Opposite page, top left: This view of the second YF-17, wearing Canadian markings, was taken while Northrop was attempting to sell the F-18L to Canada. The aircraft was also evaluated by the Spanish, although both countries eventually chose the modified version offered by McDonnell Douglas. The first YF-17 prototype 72-1569 is now preserved at Hawthorn airport, California, while 72-1570 is preserved within the USS *Alabama* memorial park at Mobile, Alabama. (Northrop)

Below: The first prototype YF-17 during its first flight with Northrop's chief test pilot, Hank Chouteau, at the controls. (Northrop)

Top right: This underside view of an F/A-18C from VX-4 shows most of the similarities in the layout between the YF-17 and the first generation of the Hornet family. One of the most visible modifications in this view is the infilling by McDonnell Douglas of the Bleed Air Ducting (BLAD) gap between the Leading Edge Extension (LEX) and the fuselage. This photo was taken in September 1992, during testing and evaluation trials for the AIM-120 Advanced Medium Range Air-to-Air Missile (AMRAAM). Although it is carrying ten AMRAAMs here, most missions currently performed by Hornets require a maximum of four. (US Navy)

Above: Current US Navy aircraft carriers use a traditional steam catapult to launch combat aircraft from their decks, but plans for the next generation of US Navy aircraft carriers include an Electro-magnetic catapult. The pilot of this F/A-18A from VFA-132 is about to feel the tremendous acceleration associated with a catapult launch. While the aircraft is secured to the catapult, its weight and the wind speed across the deck are entered into the computer for launch at an automatically predetermined height. While this happens, the pilot has his hands completely free of the controls, allowing him to literally sit back and enjoy the ride. (Key – Duncan Cubitt)

Right: An F/A-18A from VX-23 releasing five Mk.83 Low-Drag General Purpose Bombs (LDGP) bombs during Advanced Tactical Forward-Looking Infra-Red (ATFLIR) adjacent stores release tests for the F/A-18C/D in July 2002. (US Navy – Vernon Pugh)

Fighter (VFAX) that the Navy had intended to purchase. Both teams competing for the LWF contract set about designing a navalised version of each aircraft for the NACF project. Northrop had very little experience of producing fighter aircraft for the Navy and it enlisted the help of McDonnell Douglas, based at St Louis, Missouri, which had built an excellent range of jet-powered aircraft for the Navy. The two companies agreed that McDonnell Douglas would produce a navalised version of the YF-17, soon to gain the name McDonnell Douglas F-18A, for the US Navy. Northrop would act as prime subcontractor for this aircraft while continuing with the production of a land-based version of the YF-17 design, which initially

gained the F-18L designation. The second prototype, quickly repainted in a three-tone blue and green colour scheme, served as the F-18 prototype for publicity purposes and effectively became the initial trials and development aircraft for the programme.

Sadly, it was not long before this partnership began to run into problems because of differences between the two design teams. Northrop was unhappy with the McDonnell team adding extra weight to the design to make it more suitable for carrier operations. Northrop also accused its rival of trying to sell the F-18A to its own F-18L customers. Other hurdles for both companies included an initial lack of support from the Navy, and attempts by Congress to cancel the programme.

However, the aircraft survived and defeated all its critics. As a result, the Hornet was transformed from a relatively unsophisticated lightweight fighter into a true third-generation swing-role aircraft. The Hornet can perform in both air-to-air and air-to-ground modes, literally at the 'flick of a switch' during the same mission.

The F-18 was officially ordered by the Navy on May 2, 1975, though it was not until March 1, 1977, that the aircraft was named Hornet. Despite a reasonably successful export programme, the Hornet has never quite beaten off competition from its former LWF rival. The winner of this competition has become the extremely successful Lockheed Martin F-16 Fighting Falcon and has been sold to more than 22 countries, with over 4,300 built or still on order.

The F/A-18 has a proven safety record, and advantages over the F-16 include particularly the reliability of its twin-engine design. This was demonstrated during Operation Desert Storm, when several aircraft limped back to base after being hit in one engine by surface-to-air missiles. All

four models of the first generation of F/A-18s have been exported to seven countries outside the United States. Australia, Canada and Spain chose to purchase the F/A-18A and 'B models, which have all undergone upgrade programmes or are being modified to serve for another 15 years.

With the introduction of the F/A-18C/D into service, some of the earlier airframes were passed on to numerous Navy and Marine Corps reserve units, allowing them to replace the venerable McDonnell Douglas F-4 Phantom II. This model has also achieved modest export success, with aircraft exported to Finland, Kuwait, Malaysia and Switzerland. The production run for all the first-generation F/A-18s has now been terminated, the last airframe an F/A-18D completed in August 2000, with 1,479 aircraft built. Boeing has now turned its attention to the Super Hornet programme and is currently producing both the F/A-18E and F/A-18F for the US Navy. Several other countries have expressed an interest in purchasing the aircraft, including some existing Hornet operators, which have considered supplementing or even replacing their first-generation Hornet fleets.

Malaysia has even considered trading in all its current fleet as part of a plan to purchase two new fighter types. Although US Navy orders for the Super Hornet were cut from 1,000 aircraft in 1997 in favour of the Joint Strike Fighter (JSF), the US Navy still plans to purchase a combination of 548 F/A-18E and 'F models, initially to replace the Northrop Grumman F-14 Tomcat. Some units operating the F/A-18C will also convert to the Super Hornet, allowing them to re-equip with what is the first new fighter aircraft to enter fleet service since the first 'A model in 1983. However, the displaced airframes will not be retired, but reassigned to other units to even out airframe fatigue life throughout the first-generation Hornet fleet. Another export option available in these days of defence cutbacks and force reduction is the early model aircraft

Above: This Royal Australian Air Force F/A-18A was photographed climbing out for a mission during Exercise WILLOH in the late 1980s. This was a regular squadron exchange that took place until the Royal New Zealand AF air combat force was disbanded in 2001. The exercise takes its name from the participating aircraft's home bases, Williamtown and Ohakea. (RAAF via Jim Winchester collection)

Left: VFA-192 is one of three US Navy F/A-18 squadrons permanently forward deployed to the Naval Air Facility (NAF) at Atsugi, Japan. This pair of F/A-18As is seen flying past Mount Fuji during assignment to the now-retired carrier USS *Midway* in June 1989. (US Navy – Lt Cmdr T B Surbridge)

Below: Two Swiss F-18Cs seconds after releasing flares from the Tracor AN/ALE-47 chaff/flare dispensers located at the bottom of the intakes ahead of the main undercarriage. (©Swiss Air Force)

currently stored at the Aerospace Maintenance and Regeneration Center (AMARC) storage facility at Davis-Monthan AFB in Arizona.

Up to 40 aircraft that have been stored here since they were retired in the early 1990s could be given a modest upgrade similar to the F/A-18A+ re-entering service with Navy and Marine reserve units. Spain has become the only existing operator to purchase surplus aircraft – the 24 aircraft were a mix of ex-US Navy and Marine aircraft. Boeing offered the Czech Republic surplus Canadian aircraft towards the end of 2002 but due to finance problems they appear to have decided against this and have considered other types instead.

Top: An F/A-18C from the Naval Air Warfare Center at NAS Ventura County, known for many years as Point Mugu, drops a Mk.84 GBU-24 Paveway laser-guided bomb during weapons trials. The AN/AAS-38 NITE Hawk laser designator is visible here, mounted on the port side of the fuselage. (US Navy)

Above: Cross wind landing trials were performed by the first F/A-18F prototype on one of the dry lakebeds at Edwards AFB, California, in 1999. (Boeing)

Left: Six US Navy F/A-18s maintain a tight formation, while flying line astern for the company cameraman during an early operational deployment. (McDonnell Douglas)

Right: One of the better-known users of the F/A-18 is the Navy Flight Demonstration Squadron ('The Blue Angels'), based at NAS Pensacola, Florida. The team use eleven early-production aircraft modified for aerobatics with a different seat harness and the radar and M61 cannon removed. The team is seen flying over the now famous St Louis landmark, the 'Gateway to the West' arch, built in the 1960s. The arch signifies the major supply and jump-off point for settlers and wagon trains moving west. (McDonnell Douglas)

Left: A pair of F/A-18Cs from VFA-83 make a pairs take-off from Pula, Croatia, in October 2002 while taking part in Exercise Joint Wings 2002, which involved CVW-17 and the Croatian Air Force. (USN – Capt Dana Potts)

Centre left: All three F/A-18 squadrons from Carrier Air Wing 17 aboard USS *George Washington* are captured in this photograph, taken during a break from Joint Wings 2002. The formation is led by a Northrop Grumman F-14B Tomcat from VF-103 'Jolly Rogers', while a Hornet from VFA-81 'Sunliners' follows behind, accompanied by an aircraft from VFA-83 'Rampagers' on his starboard side. The final aircraft following closely behind is from VFA-34 'Blue Blasters', with two Croatian Air Force MiG-21 Fishbeds escorting. (USN – Capt Dana Potts)

Below: An F/A-18C from VFA-131 'Wildcats', with an F-14 Tomcat from the VX-9 'Evaluators' F-14 detachment, at NAS Ventura County, California, represented the Navy during Exercise Cope Snapper in October 2002. The exercise at NAS Key West, Florida, also included the 159th Fighter Wing, Louisiana ANG at New Orleans Joint Reserve Base (JRB), operating Boeing F-15A Eagles, and the 169th Fighter Squadron, South Carolina ANG with F-16C Fighting Falcons from McEntire Air National Guard Base (ANGB), South Carolina. Cope Snapper is a multi type exercise that enables both services to practise joint operations, including dissimilar air combat training. (USAF – S/Sgt Shane A Cuomo)

Right: This photo, taken during the closing stages of Operation Enduring Freedom on March 29, 2002, shows a Hornet from VFA-131 engaging full afterburner prior to being launched from one of the steam-driven catapults fitted to USS *John F Kennedy.* USN – PMA Joshua Karsten.

Right: If launching from an aircraft carrier is a heart-stopping experience, landing back on it after a long mission is quite another. This aircraft from VFA-113 'Stingers' was pictured while making an arrested landing aboard USS *Abraham Lincoln* on November 2, 2002. (USN – PH3 Lewis S Hunsaker)

Right: Sparks fly as an F/A-18C lands aboard USS *Kitty Hawk* during flight operations in April 2002. The pilot often keeps the afterburners lit until he has almost come to a complete stop. This precaution is crucial, because if he misses all four of the arrestor gear wires, he must perform a 'bolter' — go round and try again. (US Navy – PH3 John E Woods)

Right: Boeing delivered the 100th F/A-18 Super Hornet to the Navy on June 14, 2002. The aircraft, an F/A-18F, is wearing the marking of VFA-102, which commenced its conversion to the Super Hornet in 2002 and moved from the Atlantic Fleet to the Pacific Fleet in the process. (Boeing)

PROTOTYPES AND DEVELOPMENT

Among the major improvements McDonnell Douglas made to the airframe was an increase to the wing area, the designers also enlarging the nose to make room for the Hughes AN/APG-65 radar. This would be used in conjunction with the AIM-7 Sparrow missile that the Navy required the aircraft to carry. The airframe structure and undercarriage were strengthened and the nose gear gained a second wheel. The rear fuselage was lengthened slightly and a retractable in-flight refuelling probe added ahead of the cockpit canopy. The General Electric F404 engine was chosen to power the aircraft as it offered a lighter weight and more compact size than previous engines. The size of both tail fins was increased and the aircraft given nine weapons hardpoints, enabling a wide range of stores to be carried.

The first prototype F-18A made its first flight from St Louis on November 18, 1978. It performed several more test flights and went supersonic during one such flight in early December. Most prototype aircraft undertake flight test trials at the company's home base, but the Navy decided to perform all these service trials at Patuxent River, Maryland. The first prototype was transferred there to perform continued flight-testing from January 1979.

The second prototype aircraft, which made its first flight on March 12, 1979, soon joined it. All the remaining prototypes had flown by March 1980 and, as flight trials continued, McDonnell Douglas decided to promote the new aircraft by sending it to the air show and trade exhibition at Farnborough, Hampshire, UK, in September.

The aircraft chosen for this was the tenth prototype, which was also the second two-seat aircraft, then referred to as the TF-18A. The aircraft went on to make a successful appearance at the show, but the celebrations were short-lived when the aircraft crashed on the boundary of the Army Air Corps airfield at Middle Wallop, Hampshire shortly after take-off from Farnborough on September 8. An investigation revealed that a low-pressure turbine disc in the right engine had disintegrated, damaging the left engine in the process. Subsequent modifications eliminated this problem. The remaining prototypes continued the trials programme and went on to perform 2,756 test flights, amassing a total of 3,583 flying hours. After completion of the flight-testing, several prototypes were passed on to the National Aeronautics and Space Agency (NASA). Two aircraft, including the first prototype, were kept for spares use to maintain the two prototypes retained by NASA in an airworthy condition.

Right: A top-side plan view of the prototype seen in December 1978 – note the extended air brake. (McDonnell Douglas)

Below: Seen here during an early test flight near NAS Patuxent River, the first prototype aircraft is now preserved at the Naval Air Weapons Station (NAWS) at China Lake, California. (McDonnell Douglas)

Bottom: The first prototype F/A-18, captured during its maiden flight, had Navy titles on the port side and Marines on the starboard side. It was also the only aircraft to wear this gold and blue colour scheme. (McDonnell Douglas)

Above: At the time of its second flight in March 1979, the second Hornet still wore the F-18A designation. The aircraft is currently still in use with the Navy as a ground instructional airframe at the Naval Air Technical Training Center (NATTC) at Pensacola, Florida. (McDonnell Douglas)

Left: Carrier Qualifications were initially performed with the third aircraft beginning in October 1979. The aircraft performed 17 landings and 37 arrested landings over four days. Unfortunately, this aircraft was lost in a crash on March 16, 1981. (McDonnell Douglas)

Right: This July 1980 photograph of the second and seventh prototypes refuelling from a USMC Lockheed KC-130 Hercules illustrates slight differences between the two aircraft. The seventh aircraft was involved in weapons and stores separation trials during its test career, before it was struck off charge in 1987. As part of these trials, the aircraft has cameras fitted to the wing tip pylons, while the second aircraft still has the air data sensor attached to the nose. (McDonnell Douglas)

Middle right: The seventh prototype F/A-18 approaches a Naval Air Test Center (NATC) Douglas A-3 Skywarrior to conduct refuelling in February 1981. (McDonnell Douglas)

Bottom right: NASA acquired several of the F/A-18 prototypes during 1984, initially using them for aircrew proficiency and as chase aircraft for the Grumman X-29 test programme. Among the aircraft they acquired was the sixth prototype, which had been used to perform various spin recovery tests while at Patuxent River. After arriving at Dryden Flight Research Center, California on October 22, 1984, it was selected for conversion to the High (Alpha) Research Vehicle (HARV) aircraft to explore high angles of attack, making its first flight as such on April 2, 1987. The HARV programme lasted from 1987 until the aircraft was retired in 1996, split into three phases. The first of these commenced in April 1987 and were completed in 1989 after 101 test flights, with no external modifications to the airframe. However, prior to the second phase the aircraft had a thrust vectoring system installed, which included modified paddles attached in place of the exhaust nozzles and modifications to the flight control software. During the thrust vectoring trials, a spin recovery parachute was fitted to the aircraft. The second phase trials ran from January 1991 until January 1993. (NASA)

Above: Other notable changes included in the third phase were these retractable strakes, added to the nose in March 1995 to provide yaw control while the aircraft performed High Angle of Attack (AoA) manoeuvres, which left the conventional rudders ineffective. (NASA)

Above: The HARV F/A-18 flies over its base at the NASA Dryden Flight Research Center on May 29, 1996, during its final flight. The aircraft is now on display at the Virginia Air and Space Museum, at Hampton. (NASA – Jim Ross)

Left: This close-up view of the nose section shows the modified strakes added towards the end of the flight test programme. (NASA)

Above: The first prototype two-seat F/A-18 is still used by NASA as the Systems Research Aircraft (SRA) and has undergone numerous modifications to investigate new technology flight control, air data sensing and other systems. It is seen here banking over the desert near its base in July 1998. (NASA – Jim Ross)

Left: Another view of the SRA Hornet, in formation with an early-production F/A-18B during an Autonomous Free Flight (AFF) test flight on February 21, 2001 (NASA – Lori Losey)

Left: The final prototype Hornet, seen during flight testing in January 1980, in this early colour scheme, was mainly used for maintenance and engineering trials. (McDonnell Douglas)

③ F/A-18A/B

The first-production F/A-18A (161213) made its maiden flight from the McDonnell Douglas factory at St Louis, Missouri, on April 12, 1980, and after formal acceptance checks the aircraft was handed over to the Navy the following month. The first fleet replacement squadron to operate the F/A-18 was VFA-125, which commissioned at NAS Lemoore, California, on November 13, 1980. The unit received its first production aircraft in September 1981 and, once sufficient aircraft had been delivered, commenced instructor training early in 1982. On completion of this, the unit started to train the first operational aircrew to fly the new aircraft.

The first Marine Corps squadron to begin formal conversion training was VMFA-314 based at El Toro, also in California, during August 1982, and the unit regained operational status on January 7, 1983. The other squadrons from El Toro, VMFA-323 and VMFA-531, undertook conversion and were declared operational by the end of 1983. At this stage, the Marines relied on VFA-125 to train all its pilots, but set up its own training squadron – VMFAT-101, also at El Toro – in 1987. The Navy conversions were several months behind the Marines. The first of the two, which were both assigned to the Pacific Fleet, was VFA-113 (declared operational on March 29), followed by VFA-25 on July 1. Both were assigned to Carrier Air Wing 14 (CVW-14) on completion of their training and have remained with this Air Wing, deploying aboard USS *Constellation* in February 1985 for the first operational cruise of the F/A-18.

The first Atlantic Fleet squadrons began forming at Lemoore in October 1983, and until VFA-106 was set up as the East Coast Fleet Replenishment Squadron at NAS Cecil Field, Florida, on April 27, 1984, several Atlantic Fleet squadrons underwent their conversion training with VFA-125. The first of these to form was VFA-131 on October 3, quickly followed by VFA-132 on January 9, 1984. Both operated from Lemoore until they transferred to Cecil Field on February 1, 1985. Other units quickly began converting to the Hornet, including the first two Naval Reserve units VFA-303 at Lemoore on January 1, 1984, and VFA-305 at Point Mugu, California, on January 18, 1987.

Among the units to fly the Hornet, one of the shortest-lived must be VFA-161, which formed on June 17, 1986, as part of the newly-formed Carrier Air Wing 10, only to be disbanded on April 1, 1987, when financial cutbacks curtailed plans to operate 12 Air Wings.

One of the better-known units is the Naval Flight Demonstration Squadron (NFDS) 'The Blue Angels', which received some early production aircraft to replace the McDonnell Douglas A-4F Skyhawk. After an intense work-up schedule, the team performed its first display at MCAS Yuma, Arizona, on April 25, 1987. The Navy eventually received 371 F/A-18A and 39 F/A-18Bs, with deliveries finally ending in 1987. With newer Hornets entering service, some of the first-generation aircraft were passed on to other Navy and Marine reserve units during the 1990s, while some of the older airframes were retired and placed into storage at the Naval Air Depot (NAD), North Island, California. While the Navy and Marines initially avoided a modest upgrade to first-generation aircraft, they eventually changed their plans and 28 Navy Reserve F/A-18As underwent modification to F/A-18A+, which brought them up to a similar standard to the F/A-18C.

The Marines also put 24 aircraft through this upgrade programme and plans to modify a total of 76 F/A-18As to serve with two active and four reserve squadrons. The F/A-18A+ upgrade includes the newer AN/APG-73 radar, together with a Rockwell/Collins AN/ARC-210 (V) jam

Above: Early F/A-18s were delivered to the Navy and Marines in this colour scheme, illustrated on the second-production aircraft photographed while in service with VX-4. (McDonnell Douglas)

Below: The US Navy originally planned to purchase a reconnaissance version of the Hornet, giving the manufacturer authorisation to begin a development programme in 1982. The second-production F/A-18 was used in the F/A-18R trials programme, which began in 1984. Both this and the first prototype aircraft received a removable pallet fitted in the space normally occupied by the M61 cannon. The first flight of an aircraft fitted with the reconnaissance pallet was on August 15, 1984, but the programme was eventually shelved, with both aircraft being delivered to NASA. (McDonnell Douglas)

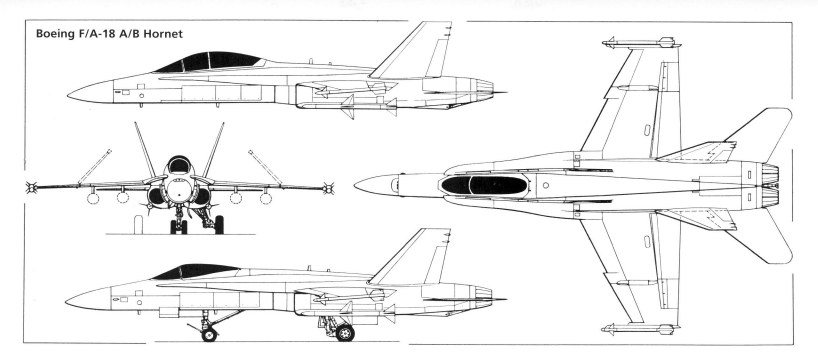

Boeing F/A-18 A/B Hornet

Left: The sixth F/A-18A seen during early weapons trials in September 1981. It was subsequently written off in a crash while operating with the Naval Air Test Center on May 2, 1983.
(McDonnell Douglas)

resistant radio and the AN/APX-111X (V) combined Identification Friend or Foe (IFF) interrogator/transponder. Other features include a Smiths Industries' AN/AYQ-9 stores management system and a night vision compatible cockpit. The General Dynamics' XN-8 mission computer and digital display indicator have been upgraded.

The upgrades will give the aircraft the ability to use the AN/AAS-38B Forward Looking Infra Red (FLIR) pod and carry most of the weapons that later models use, including the AIM-120 AMRAAM and the AGM-154 Joint Stand Off Weapon (JSOW).

Apart from the remaining Hornets that serve with both the active and reserve Navy and Marines squadrons, some still serve with various Naval test and evaluation units. Several early-production aircraft also still serve with NASA as chase aircraft for experimental types, and for a wide variety of test programmes. Some are used as training airframes aboard aircraft carriers decks while they are in their homeport.

Canada announced an order for 138 F/A-18s on April 10, 1980. Of these, 98 airframes were F/A-18As and the remaining 40 were F/A-18Bs. It was the first export order for the Hornet and makes Canada the largest user of the Hornet outside the United States. Canadian Hornets use the designation CF-188, which is used as the basis for the

F/A-18A SPECIFICATION DATA	
Length overall:	56ft 0in (17.07m)
Wingspan:	37ft 6in (11.43m)
Wingspan, over missiles:	40ft 4¾in (12.31m)
Width, wings folded:	27ft 6in (8.38m)
Height:	15ft 3½in (4.66m)
Tailplane span:	21ft 7¾in (6.58m)
Empty weight:	23,050lb (10,455kg)
Maximum internal fuel:	10,860lb (4,926kg)
External fuel:	6,732lb (3,053kg)
Maximum external stores load:	17,000lb (7,710kg)
Maximum level speed:	More than Mach 1.8
Maximum level speed, intermediate power:	More than Mach 1.0
Approach speed:	134 knots (248km/h -154mph)
Take-off run:	1,400ft (427m)
Combat ceiling:	50,000ft (15,240m)
Combat radius, attack mission:	More than 575nm (1,065km)
Combat radius, fighter mission:	More than 400nm (740km)
Ferry range, unrefuelled:	More than 2,000nm (3,706km)
Armament:	One M61 cannon with 570 rounds,
	plus air-to-air and air-to-ground
	weapons
Powerplant:	Almost all first-generation Hornets fitted with
two General Electric F404-GE-400s, each producing 16,000lb (71.2kN) thrust	

Left: An F/A-18B from VFA-125, the first operational Fleet Replacement Squadron during carrier qualifications in July 1983. (McDonnell Douglas)

Below: This Hornet still wears the F-18A designation and the early colour scheme during a test flight. (McDonnell Douglas)

Bottom: VX-4 based at NAWS China Lake used several early production aircraft to continue weapons trials. This aircraft is now preserved at NAS Lemoore. (McDonnell Douglas)

Right: VMFA-314 has flown many types since it was formed at Cherry Point, North Carolina, on October 1, 1943, including the Vought F4U Corsair flown during the invasion of Okinawa in May 1945. The unit became VMFA (AW)-314 when it re-equipped with the Douglas F-4D Skyray in 1957, and converted to the McDonnell Douglas F-4B Phantom II in 1961. It continued to fly several versions of the Phantom until converting to the F/A-18A. One of the squadron's aircraft is seen taking the arrestor wire during carrier qualifications in July 1983. (McDonnell Douglas)

Middle right: A pair of F/A-18As from the first operational Pacific Fleet squadrons, VFA-113 in the foreground and VFA-25 behind. Both flew the LTV A-7E Corsair II prior to the Hornet. Here, both pilots await the signal to launch from USS *Constellation* while the ship was deployed on a WestPac cruise in October 1988. (McDonnell Douglas)

Bottom: VFA-136 was among the first three operational Atlantic Fleet Hornet squadrons. Unlike VFA-131 and VFA-132, which had been inactive for a number of years, the 'Knighthawks' had no previous operational history. The unit participated in numerous exercises in 1990, before taking part in Operation Desert Shield during 1990. (USN – Lt Cmdr John Leenhouts)

aircraft's serial number, although they are now more commonly referred to as CF-18s. The aircraft were purchased to replace the McDonnell F-101 Voodoo, the Lockheed F-104 Starfighter and, later, the Canadair CF-5 Freedom Fighter. Canadian aircraft were fitted with provision to carry LAU-5003 rocket pods, and a different Instrumented Landing System (ILS) to the US Navy version. They were also the first aircraft to be fitted with a spotlight on the portside for identification of aircraft at night.

The first aircraft, CF-18B 188901, flew on July 29, 1982, with deliveries to the Air Force commencing on October 25. No.410 Squadron became the first unit to convert to the aircraft at Cold Lake, Alberta. Once the aircraft had entered operational service, they assumed responsibility for Canada's contribution to the defence of North America and Canada as part of the North American Air Defense system (NORAD) operated by both countries. The first of the aircraft was delivered in October 1982 and the last in September 1988. Canada initially planned to refer to its two-seaters as CF-188Ds (D for Dual), given that all trainers have this designation, although this was later changed to the CF-18B in line with the American designation for two-seat aircraft.

Eighty Canadian Hornets will receive colour liquid-crystal flat-panel cockpit displays to replace the current 1970s-style monochrome displays, starting in 2005. The contract to develop the new systems was awarded to Boeing in July 2002. It has subcontracted Litton Systems Canada to undertake the development work for the project, part of a wider upgrade package for the CF-18 fleet due to be completed in 2007. The RAAF also plans to incorporate this upgrade on its aircraft, and it is available to both Spain and the USA, which may add it to the first generation of Hornets. Australia became the second export customer for the aircraft when it signed a contract in October 1981. The order was for 75 Hornets, of which 57 were 'A models and the remaining 18 'Bs, once the Hornets entered service they began to replace Dassault Mirage IIIOs.

The first two F/A-18Bs were built at St Louis, and were delivered to the RAAF on May 17, 1985, while the remaining aircraft were assembled from kits by Aerospace Technologies of Australia (ASTA) at Avalon. The first of

Below: Another unit that converted from the A-7E was VFA-15, which commenced type conversion on October 1, 1986. This four-ship was photographed while the unit worked up to operational strength in early 1987. (McDonnell Douglas)

Bottom: The 'World Famous Golden Dragons' of VFA-192 moved to Japan after conversion to the F/A-18 in 1986 and have remained there ever since, initially operating from USS *Midway*. One of the unit's aircraft is seen passing the Mihara volcano on Ō-shima Island off central Japan. The squadron currently uses NAF Atsugi as its home base. (USN – Lt Cmdr T Surbridge)

Above: One of the F/A-18As assigned to the Pacific Missile Test Center at NAS Point Mugu, California, firing an AIM-120 AMRAAM during early trials for the new missile. At the time of writing, this aircraft was in service with NASA as N850NA. (USN)

Right: VMFA-312 converted to the F/A-18A in 1988 after operating the F-4 Phantom, the squadron subsequently re-equipped with the F/A-18C. However, the 'Checkertails' have now exchanged these for the upgraded F/A-18A+. The aircraft in this photo – 163166 – is a late-production F/A-18A and is carrying an AGM-88 High-Speed Anti-Radiation Missile (HARM). (McDonnell Douglas)

Right: The US Navy Test Pilots School is one of the better-known units based at Patuxent River. It operates four early-production F/A-18Bs. (Key – Malcolm English)

Right: On January 1, 1992, another well-known unit at Pax River – the Naval Air Test Center – was amalgamated with several other test and development centres to form the Naval Air Warfare Center-Aircraft Division (NAWC-AD). The unit operates a large fleet of Hornets and Super Hornets. In this picture, one of the unit's F/A-18As crosses the runway threshold prior to landing. (Key – Malcolm English)

Left: Several Hornet squadrons have been disbanded due to defence cutbacks during the 1990s, one of the unlucky units being the 'Privateers' of VFA-132 who were assigned to Carrier Air Wing 6 aboard USS *Forrestal* while taking part in Exercise Display Determination in the Mediterranean. VFA-132 disbanded on April 1, 1992, and CVW-6 followed shortly afterwards, while the *Forrestal* was decommissioned on September 30, 1993. (Key – Duncan Cubitt)

Left: The other squadron assigned to CVW-6 was VFA-137, which transferred to the Pacific Fleet a year after this photo was taken in September 1991. One of the unit's F/A-18s makes a sprightly departure from the *Forrestal*. (Key – Duncan Cubitt)

Below: The US Naval Reserve originally had two Reserve Carrier Air Wings (CVWR) until one of these, CVWR-30 on the West Coast, was disbanded. CVWR-20, based at Atlanta, Georgia, has four Navy and one Marine F/A-18A squadrons assigned to it. VFA-201 is normally based at Fort Worth Joint Reserve Base (JRB), Texas, and the unit occasionally operates from a carrier during training, but it was assigned to CVW-8 in late 2002 aboard USS *Theodore Roosevelt*. (USN – PH1 James Foehl)

these made its first flight on February 26, 1985, with the final aircraft handed over in May 1990. Australian aircraft are primarily used in the air defence role and have taken part in various exercises, including a number of Integrated Air Defense Systems (IADS) exercises. These were held in conjunction with the air forces of Malaysia and Singapore, together with the Royal New Zealand Air Force while it still had an air combat force, and occasionally the Royal Air Force and Royal Navy. The first RAAF F/A-18 to undergo the first phase of the Hornet Upgrade (HUG) was rolled out at RAAF Williamtown on September 7, 2000. The HUG programme consists of the installation of an ARC-210 UHF/VHF radio and upgrading of supporting systems, and replacement of the IFF system with a combined interrogator and transponder. At the same time, an embedded Global Positioning System (GPS) has been added to the Inertial Navigation System (INS). Upgrades have also been made to the XN-8+ mission computers multiplex databus and additional wiring has been added

Right: VFA-203's aircraft have been converted to F/A-18A+ standard and this pair was pictured visiting NAS Lemoore in October 2002. (Key – Mark Nicholls)

Below: Four of VFA-204's F/A-18As waiting on the flightline during a detachment to NAS Oceana Virginia in August 2001. The unit is due to convert to the F/A-18A+ and is normally based at New Orleans JRB, Louisiana. (Jim Winchester)

Bottom: 1992 photograph of F-18A cockpit of a Blue Angels aircraft. (US Navy/John Bennett)

Right: The Naval Fighter Weapons School (NFWS) based at Miramar, California, and famously known as Top Gun, trained fleet aircrew in aerial combat tactics. The unit received its first F/A-18 in 1987. During the 1990s some aircraft were painted in colour schemes similar to those worn by Soviet fighter aircraft. (USN – PM1 Mahlon K Miller)

Right: Several training units, including the Naval Fighter Weapons School and the Naval Strike Warfare Center (NSWC) at Fallon, Nevada, were combined to form the Naval Strike Air Warfare Center (NSAWC) in 1996. The larger unit, now based at Fallon, gained some aircraft from the resident VFA-127. When it disbanded, several of that unit's aircraft were painted in this desert camouflage scheme. (Key – Alan Warnes)

Right: The last active fleet unit to operate the F/A-18A was VFA-97 and it was due to operate this until 2004. One of the squadron's aircraft waits on the flightline at Lemoore prior to a mission in October 1996. It is wearing special markings for both the squadron boss and the Carrier Air Wing commander. (Key – Alan Warnes)

Bottom: China Lake is the home of VX-9, which was created from the merger of the fighter test unit VX-4 and the strike attack unit VX-5 in the 1990s. (Key – Steve Fletcher)

Right: The US Navy still has about 40 airframes in long-term storage at the Aerospace Maintenance and Regeneration Center (AMARC) at Davis-Monthan, Arizona. Other aircraft stored here are sprayed with a white protective covering called Spraylat, while several of the F/A-18s are kept in these large storage bags. Among the first aircraft to enter storage was F/A-18A 161710, which arrived in June 1994. It was among some of the older examples that were struck off charge during 2001, as the prospect of the aircraft being offered for export seemed to have receded. (Key – Dave Allport)

Right: Some early-production Hornets have been put on display in museums or as base gate guardians. One such aircraft, 162454, is kept in the Oceana Air Park. It was restored to display condition after colliding in mid-air with another F/A-18A on April 23, 1996, while serving with VFC-12. (Jim Winchester)

Below: Another preserved aircraft, 161961, once flew with 'The Blue Angels' and is currently kept outside at the National Museum of Naval Aviation at Pensacola, Florida. (Dave Willis)

for a new Air Combat Manoeuvring System (ACMI) pod system.

Eight aircraft were scheduled to arrive at Williamtown by the end of 2000, with the 71 surviving aircraft scheduled to undergo conversion by the end of June 2002. The second phase of the HUG programme began in March 2002, when the first airframes were handed over for work to commence at Williamtown. These improvements include replacement of the AN/APG-65 radar with the newer AN/APG-73, bringing the aircraft to almost the same standard as late model 'C airframes. This process is due to be completed by mid-2003. The RAAF is also planning some structural improvements, scheduled

to be completed by 2006. These will ensure the aircraft will serve until its planned retirement date of 2012.

Spain became the last country to purchase first-generation Hornets after it signed a Letter of offer and Acceptance (LOA) in May 1983. The order was for 72 aircraft, comprising 60 'A models and 12 'Bs, purchased to operate with, and eventually replace, the McDonnell Douglas F-4C Phantom II and Dassault Mirage IIIs. The first deliveries to the Spanish Air Force began in January 1986 and the final aircraft was handed over in July 1990. Spanish aircraft went through an upgrade between 1992 and 1994 to update internal wiring and other systems, as well as increasing the memory of the flight control

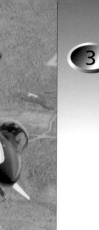

Above: NASA F/A-18s have flown as chase aircraft for the Deutsche Aerospace/Rockwell International X-31 Enhanced Fighter Maneuverability (EFM) demonstrator. (NASA)

Right: Aviation ordnance personnel check new weapons before attaching them to aircraft from Carrier Air Wing 3 (CVW-3) during a conventional loading exercise on the flight deck of USS *Harry S Truman*. Several Hornets are painted up in full-colour unit markings, including the F/A-18A+ from VMFA-115, which became the first unit to deploy the aircraft operationally aboard USS *Harry S Truman* in November 2002. (USN – PM3 Danny Ewing Jr)

Right: Prior to re-equipping with the F/A-18 in 1984, NASA used the Lockheed F-104 Starfighter both as chase aircraft and for performing other research and test duties. This formation, led by a Northrop T-38A Talon, was to celebrate test pilot Bill Dana's first flight in a Starfighter in 1960 and was photographed shortly before the F-104s were finally retired in 1990. (NASA)

Below right: Several of the NASA F/A-18As have been retired from active service. Two of these aircraft, 841 and the original aircraft that carried the serial 843, were transferred to the Naval Weapons Center at China Lake during the late 1980s for use as range targets. NASA donated another aircraft, 842, to the Lancaster municipal baseball stadium in California in March 1997. (Key – Duncan Cubitt)

Left: An F/A-18A from VX-9 taxies out to the runway for another mission at NAWS China Lake in April 1997. (Key – Steve Fletcher)

computer. Spain also obtained 24 surplus airframes from Naval Air Systems Command (NAVAIR), of which eleven were stored at the AMARC facility at Davis-Monthan AFB, Arizona. These were moved by road for refurbishment while the remainder were taken from active service and ferried to NAS North Island. The aircraft underwent some upgrade work prior to delivery, bringing them up to almost the same standards as other Spanish aircraft. The contracts were signed in September 1995 and the airframes were delivered at a rate of six per year, starting in December 1995, with the last arriving in December 1998. With the addition of these, the Spanish received a total of 96 aircraft, while also included in the deal were 51 new F404 engines. EADS CASA is upgrading the survivors of the original 72 airframes, although the additional aircraft purchased during the 1990s will not be upgraded.

Above: No.75 Squadron previously flew Dassault Mirage IIIOs from Darwin Northern Territories until it disbanded in May 1988, receiving its first Hornets the same month. The Hornets in Exercise Lima Bersatu operated alongside Malaysian and Singaporean AF F-5Es and RAF Tornado F.3s from No.29 Squadron that were part of Exercise Golden Eagle 88, a 66-day circumnavigation of the world by RAF fighters. They were pitched against Australian General Dynamics F-111, Malaysian AF Aermacchi MB-339s, Singaporean AF Douglas A-4 Skyhawks and Royal Navy BAe Sea Harriers. The squadron moved to a new air base at Tindal shortly after the exercise finished and have remained there ever since.
(Rolls-Royce)

Right: Australian F/A-18As from the newly-reformed 75 Squadron took part in Exercise Lima Bersatu in September 1988. The exercise involved Malaysia, Singapore, New Zealand and the United Kingdom, which together with Australia, form part of the Five-Power Defence Arrangement (FPDA).
(Key Archive)

Right: No.409 Squadron was originally assigned to NORAD, but transferred to the 1st Canadian Air Group (CAG) at Baden Soellingen in what was then West Germany. They were joined by 421 and 439 Squadrons, with the wing eventually operating a total of 56 aircraft by the end of 1988. The three squadrons were disbanded after Operation Desert Storm, the last aircraft returning to Canada in early 1993, and Baden closed later the same year. (McDonnell Douglas)

Top: All Canadian Hornets wear English and French titles either side of the roundel. Canada is also the only export customer to paint false canopies under its aircraft. (Key – Duncan Cubitt)

Above: The first four EF-18Bs for Ala 15 (Wing) during the delivery flight from St Louis to Zaragoza, Spain, on July 10, 1986. All the Spanish Hornets originally wore the squadron number as part of a coding system, so three aircraft belong to 151 Escuadrón (Squadron), while the nearest aircraft was assigned to 152 Escuadrón. (McDonnell Douglas)

Left: A pair of Ala 12 EF-18As captured on finals to land at RAF Waddington in June 2001. (Key – Steve Fletcher)

F/A-18C/D

had to wait until June 1989 to re-equip with the aircraft.

After McDonnell Douglas produced 137 standard model F/A-18Cs and 31 F/A-18Ds, it switched to production of the Night Attack version for the Navy. The first airframe built to this standard was an F/A-18C (163985), while the other aircraft converted to serve as the prototype for the Marines was the first-production F/A-18D (163434). Both flew for the first time on May 6, 1988. The aircraft went through an extensive test programme prior to first deliveries to VFA-146 beginning on December 13, 1989, shortly after the first-production Night Attack F/A-18D (163986) had arrived at the Naval Air Test Center at Patuxent River in November 1989. The Marines received their first Night Attack F/A-18D on May 11, 1990. Although the mission-capable rear cockpit on these aircraft has no control column or throttles, they could be converted back to dual if they were needed for training purposes.

McDonnell Douglas also delivered the 1,000th aircraft, F/A-18D (164237) to VMFA (AW)-242 at El Toro on April 18, 1991. Additional changes were made to the engine and from early 1991, F/A-18Cs were delivered fitted with the General Electric F404-GE-402 Enhanced Performance Engine (EPE) that gives the aircraft an extra 10% of thrust. One of the major improvements was the ability to carry the AIM-120 AMRAAM as well as the AIM-7. The missile was cleared for carriage on the F/A-18C in September 1993.

The radar fitted to earlier Hornets had undergone various upgrades throughout the 1980s until its growth potential had been used up, so a new upgraded version was developed using the antenna and transmitter from the APG-65, coupled to new entirely new electronics. The new version began flight testing in 1992 and new F/A-18Cs with the upgraded APG-73 were delivered to VFA-146 and VFA-147 in May 1994. The final production total for both versions of the Night Attack Hornet amounted to 330 F/A-18Cs and 130 F/A-18Ds, with the last 60 completed as F/A-18D Reconnaissance Capable (RC) aircraft.

Above: The first-production F/A-18C lifts off from the runway at St Louis for its first flight on September 3, 1987, with test pilot Glen Larson at the controls. The aircraft was written off in a crash while serving with VFA-81 on October 2, 1989. (McDonnell Douglas)

Below: Day and night views of cockpit of F/A-18D. The cockpit dominated by the three multi-functional colour display screens. (McDonnell Douglas)

Although the new model F/A-18 was essentially similar in appearance to earlier production aircraft, it had several external differences due to the installation of additional antennae for new Electronic Countermeasures (ECM) systems. These were fitted on the nose and on the nosewheel undercarriage doors of the aircraft, while others were added to the spine and both fins. All the other changes were internal – some changes were made to avionics systems inside the cockpit, such as the mission computer, which was given an expanded memory. Some internal improvements were made to the F404 engine after a spate of engine fires in high-timed engines that burnt through to the airframe, resulting in several aircraft losses in 1987.

The first F/A-18C built (163427) flew on September 3, 1987, and was delivered to the Naval Weapons Center at China Lake on September 23, 1987, but the fleet units

The Marines' need for a reconnaissance platform increased with the retirement of the McDonnell Douglas RF-4B Phantom II in 1990. However, a previous proposal to purchase the RF-18D was abandoned as part of defence cutbacks that left the Marines without a suitable reconnaissance aircraft. The Marines made a decision to use the Advanced Tactical Airborne Reconnaissance System (ATARS), then being developed by the US Air Force, in the F/A-18D. Although the Air Force subsequently cancelled the programme, the Marines decided to continue and took on the development programme in 1994. Initial trials were performed in a modified drop tank fitted to the first-production F/A-18D. The ATARS system is fitted into the same pallet system originally tried on the first prototype Hornet and an early-production F/A-18A back in 1984. Although the trials programme had not been completed, the Marines deployed the system in two ATARS-capable F/A-18Ds from VMFA (AW)-332, which commenced operations from Taszar air base in Hungary on May 26, 1999, flying missions during Operation Allied Force.

Export orders for the second generation were slightly better, although one was cancelled due to financial reasons. Kuwait had begun searching for a new fighter aircraft during the late 1980s, and the three contenders for the order were the Dassault Mirage 2000, McDonnell Douglas with the F/A-18C/D and the Panavia Tornado F.3. Kuwait eventually opted to purchase the F/A-18 to replace its mixed fleet of Dassault Mirage F1CKs and McDonnell Douglas A-4KU Skyhawks, and placed an order in September 1988 for 40 aircraft comprising 32 F/A-18Cs and eight F/A-18Ds. The original delivery plans were delayed due to the Iraqi invasion in August 1990 and were put on hold until the end of Operation Desert Storm. The first aircraft, F/A-18D (441), completed its maiden flight on September 19, 1991, and the deliveries began when three flew to Kuwait in January 1992, with the last aircraft delivered in August 1993.

Left: One of the first-production F/A-18Ds to enter service with VFA-125 climbs over the desert for the company cameraman in October 1989.
(McDonnell Douglas)

Above: The first F/A-18D served as the trials airframe for the Night Attack Hornet programme and is seen here during an early test flight over Missouri farmland in May 1988.
(McDonnell Douglas)

Left: Steam emerges from the catapult as a VFA-86 F/A-18C is launched from USS *America*, cruising in the Mediterranean during Exercise Display Determination in September 1989, shortly after converting to this version of the Hornet. (Key – Duncan Cubitt)

Centre: One of VMFA (AW)-121s seen over Kuwait City shortly after the end of Operation Desert Storm. (McDonnell Douglas)

Bottom: VMFA-312 converted to the F/A-18C in August 1991, becoming operational in November the same year. The unit continued to operate the version until it was re-equipped with the upgraded F/A-18A+ in 2001. Both aircraft carry a single AGM-88 HARM. (McDonnell Douglas)

Top: The F/A-18C used as the trials aircraft for the General Electric F404-GE-402 Enhanced Performance Engine (EPE) waits its turn to refuel while a Northrop Grumman F-14 Tomcat approaches the tanker aircraft during flight trials for the uprated engine in November 1991.
(USN – Vernon Pugh)

Centre: One of the Hornets VFA-81 used to shoot down a Mikoyan MiG-21 during Operation Desert Storm appeared in the static park at the Farnborough Air Show in September 1992, still wearing a small kill symbol on the nose.
(Key – Duncan Cubitt)

Bottom: Before it received a full unit complement of Night Attack F/A-18Ds, VMFA (AW)-533 operated a mix of F/A-18C and D model Hornets.
(McDonnell Douglas)

Finland was seeking an aircraft to replace its fleet of Mikoyan MiG-21 Fishbeds and SAAB 35 Drakens in 1989, and conducted evaluation flights with several different types in 1991 and 1992. These included the Dassault Mirage 2000-5, General Dynamics F-16, Mikoyan MiG-29 Fulcrum and finally the SAAB Gripen. The F/A-18 was chosen as the winner on May 6, 1992, although the Finnish planned to operate it as an air defence aircraft and chose to use the F-18 designation. An order for 64 aircraft was placed on June 5, 1992, with the first seven aircraft – all F-18Ds – being built at St Louis, the first making its first flight on April 21, 1995. The first deliveries commenced when four aircraft flew to Pirrkala air base in southern Finland on November 7, 1995. The first aircraft assembled in Finland by Finavitec (formerly Valmet) was delivered on June 28, 1996, while the final aircraft was delivered in August 2000.

Malaysia placed an order for eight F/A-18Ds on June 29, 1993, with the first aircraft M45-01 making its maiden flight on February 1, 1997. Deliveries commenced when the first four aircraft arrived in Malaysia on March 19, 1997, and the final aircraft were delivered on August 31 the same year.

During the 1980s, the Swiss Air Force began searching for a new fighter to replace its fleet of Mirage IIIS and to supplement the Northrop F-5E Tiger IIs that were flown in

the air defence role. Contenders under consideration included the General Dynamics F-16C, McDonnell Douglas F/A-18C and both the Dassault Mirage 2000 and Rafale. The SAAB JAS 39 Gripen was also examined, along with the IAI Lavi and Northrop F-20. Both of these were ruled out at an early stage, as they never completed their respective development programmes, while the Rafale was deemed far too expensive.

On March 7, 1988, the Swiss MoD announced that the F-16 and the F/A-18 were shortlisted for a fly-off competition at Payerne. The Hornet quickly showed it was the better of the two and the government announced its success on October 3, 1988. However, this sparked a political row and Dassault, supported by a member of the Swiss political establishment, tried to promote the newer Mirage 2000-5. The Air Force insisted it preferred the F/A-18, and as a result the government was forced to turn to the Swiss population, asking them to vote on their choice for the new fighter. The F/A-18 was declared the winner and the Swiss Government signed an order in June 1993 for 34 aircraft, comprising 26 single-seat and eight two-seat aircraft that the Swiss Air Force refer to as F-18C and F-18D. The first two were built at St Louis, with the first aircraft F-18D (J-5231) making its first flight on January

Above: This F/A-18C from VFA-22 carries a Mk.83 1,000lb (454kg) laser-guided bomb on the port wing. It also carries an air combat manoeuvring instrumentation pod in place of an AIM-9 and an empty Multiple Ejection Rack on the starboard wing.
(McDonnell Douglas)

Right: An F/A-18C from VX-9 touches down on the China Lake runway in April 1997. The aircraft has photographic calibration markings applied for weapons separation tests.
(Key – Steve Fletcher)

Below: VFA-113 was one of the first units to become operational with the F/A-18A and later the F/A-18C. The squadron operated this multi-coloured Commander Air Group (CAG) bird in 1998.
(Boeing)

Left, centre and bottom:
The Atlantic and Pacific
Fleet Replacement
Squadron (FRS) at Oceana
and Lemoore provides air-
crew training for the Navy
and occasionally Marines,
and as a result their air-
craft often wear both serv-
ices' titles on the fuselage.
Both the 'Rough Raiders'
of VFA-125 and the
'Gladiators' of VFA-106,
which perform the Atlantic
Fleet FRS tasking, often
participate at air shows
across the USA.
Left (Boeing)
Centre (Key – Duncan
Cubitt)
Bottom (Key – Steve
Fletcher)

Above: VFA-136 over the Persian Gulf, March 1992. (US Navy/cw02 Tony Alleyne)

Left: This F/A-18C from VFA-82 wears the CVW-1 titles during the same cruise aboard the JFK in February 2000. Both VFA-82 and VFA-86 are currently based at MCAS Beaufort, North Carolina. (Tony Holmes)

Left: All the units assigned to Carrier Air Wing 14 participated in Exercise Northern Edge in the Gulf of Alaska in April 2002. Here, an F/A-18C from VFA 113 undergoes a pre-flight inspection aboard USS *Abraham Lincoln* on April 21, 2002. (USN – PMA Mason Cavazos)

20, 1996, while the first single-seat F-18C (J-5001) flew on April 8 that year. All the remaining aircraft were manufactured from kits supplied to the Swiss Aircraft and Systems company at Emmen.

The first Swiss-built aircraft made its debut flight on October 3, with deliveries to the Air Force commencing in early 1997 with the last aircraft, F-18C J-5026, being handed over on December 2, 1999. Switzerland originally expressed an interest in purchasing additional F/A-18s to supplement its remaining 33 airframes, though this would prove difficult as the F/A-18C/D is not in production.

Thailand placed an order for eight F/A-18s in 1996, originally intending to purchase a mix of four F/A-18Cs and four F/A-18Ds, scheduled for delivery in 1999. This order was cancelled for financial reasons, although the aircraft were already under construction at the time and were taken over by the US Government and completed as F/A-18Ds, entering service with the Marines in 2000. The last of these was delivered to VMFA (AW)-121 on August 25, marking the end of production of the first-generation Hornet.

Above: One of VFA-83's F/A-18Cs launches from the flight deck of USS *George Washington* while the 'Rampagers' and other units from CVW-17 were conducting combat missions in support of Operation Enduring Freedom in August 2002. (USN – PM3 T J Talarico)

Right: Groundcrew direct an F/A-18C into position inside the hangar deck aboard USS *Harry S Truman* in December 2002. (USN – PM1 Michael W Pendergrass)

Right: An F/A-18C from the Golden Dragons of VFA-192 moments from touching down on the flight deck of USS *Kitty Hawk* during carrier qualifications in March 2002. The unit was working up for an upcoming deployment later in 2002. *Kitty Hawk* is currently the only permanently forward-deployed aircraft carrier operating from Yokosuka, Japan, and is due for retirement in 2008. (USN – PM3 John E Woods).

Above: VFA-151 currently operates within Carrier Air Wing 2, aboard USS *Constellation* that was due to be retired following its last WestPac cruise in 2003. This will leave the Navy with just two conventionally-powered aircraft carriers.
(Tony Holmes)

Left: When the F/A-18 entered service with the Navy in 1983, the Northrop Grumman F-14 Tomcat was operated purely as a long-range fleet defence fighter, while the Hornet complemented and finally replaced both the Grumman A-6 Intruder and LTV A-7 Corsair II. The F-14 fleet was modified to undertake some of the duties performed by Intruders in the 1990s and as a result have often provided laser designation for Hornets over Afghanistan and Iraq. An F/A-18C from VFA-27 escorts an F-14 Tomcat from VF-154 over the Sea of Japan while conducting routine flight operations on March 8, 2001.
(USN – PO3 Alex C Witte)

Below: Two F/A-18Cs from the 'Knighthawks' of VFA-136 return to USS *John F Kennedy* on March 31, 2002, after conducting a combat mission over international waters and in the skies over Afghanistan in support of Operation Enduring Freedom.
(USN – Capt William E Gortney)

Above: VFA-81 is one of several F/A-18C units due to convert to the Super Hornet. A conversion timetable announced in early 2003 stated that the 'Sunliners' would relinquish their first-generation Hornets in favour of the F/A-18E in 2005. This may change with the planned integration of Marine and Navy Air Wings that was announced in 2002. One front-line unit operating F/A-18Cs may be disestablished, along with a reserve unit from each service. (USN – Capt Dana Potts)

Right: McDonnell Douglas used this new-build Marine Corps F/A-18D for the Finnish AF Hornet evaluation flight trials from Halli in February 1992. During the evaluation, it wore SF codes on the tail referring to Suomi/Finland. (Jyrki Laukkanen)

Right: First F-18 for the Finnish Air Force on intial flight April 21, 1995 out of Lambert International Airport. The aircraft was flown by MCDD test piot Fred Madenwald and Navy Lt Cdr Dave Stuart. Most Finnish F-18Cs were delivered in kit form and after final assembly test-flown from Halli.

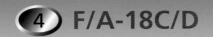

Left: The first Finnish unit to re-equip with the F-18 was 21 Squadron (Hävittäjälentolaivue/HävL Lv) at the joint civil and military airfield at Tampere-Pirrkala. One of the first aircraft to be delivered is seen flying over the city of Tampere in March 1996. (Jyrki Laukkanen)

Left and below: A number of Royal Air Force aircraft attended an international air show at Tampere-Pirrkala in June 1998, and HävLLv 21 was on hand to escort the visiting aircraft to the airfield. Among the types that appeared were a pair of BAE Harrier GR.7s from No.1(F) Squadron, then based at RAF Wittering, Cambridgeshire, and a pair of Panavia Tornado GR.1s from No.9 Squadron, formerly based at RAF Bruggen, Germany. (Jyrki Laukkanen)

Above: The Finnish Air Force Flight Test Center (Koelentokeskus/KoeLntK) is based at Halli and performs various test and trials work with several F-18s. (Jyrki Laukkanen)

Top right: The first three F/A-18s for Kuwait are seen during their delivery flight in January 1992, shortly before taking on fuel from a US Air Force McDonnell Douglas KC-10 Extender. (McDonnell Douglas)

Centre right: The Kuwait Air Force sent three F/A-18s to participate at the International Air Tattoo at RAF Fairford, Gloucestershire, in July 1993. (Jim Winchester)

Right: The final four F/A-18Ds for delivery to Malaysia sit on the ramp at St Louis prior to departing in August 1997. (Boeing)

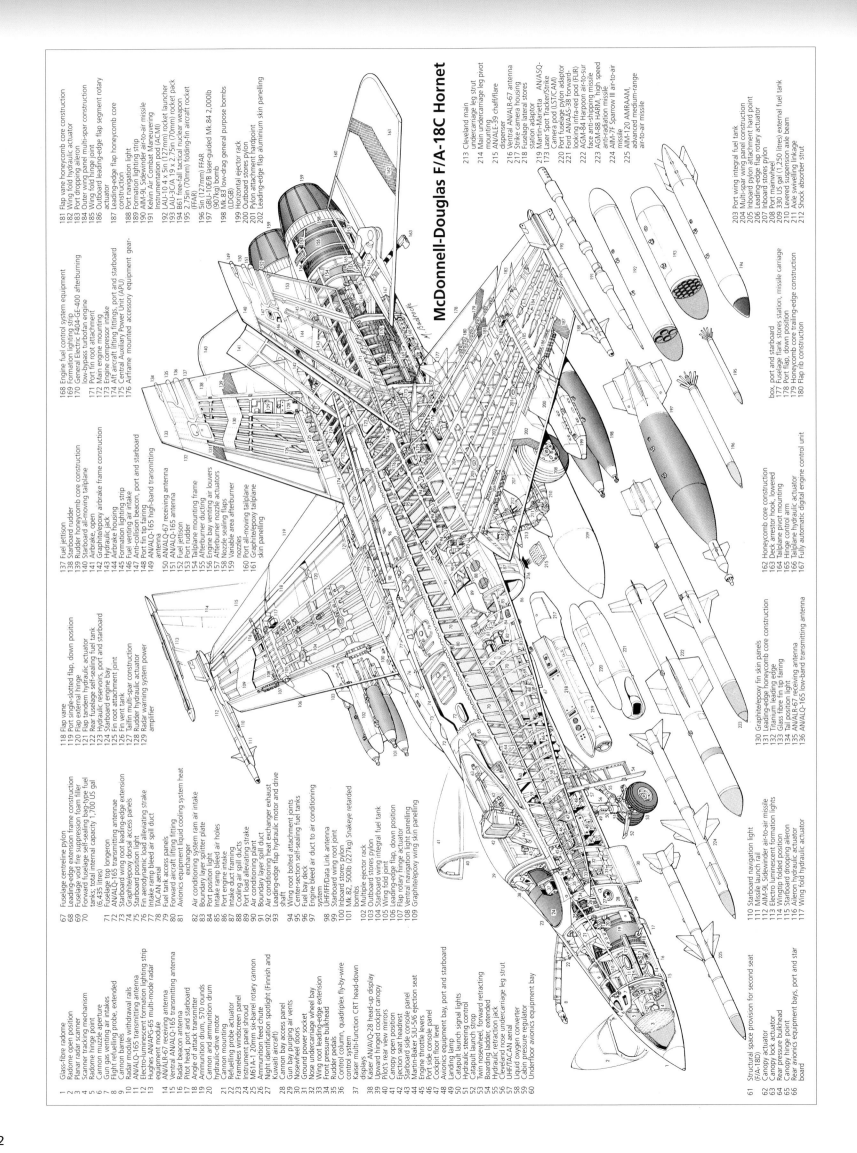

McDonnell-Douglas F/A-18C Hornet

1 Glass-fibre radome
2 Radome open position
3 Planar radar scanner
4 Carrier tracking mechanism
5 Radome hinge
6 Gun gas venting air intakes
7 Cannon muzzle aperture
8 Flight refuelling probe, extended
9 Cannon barrels
10 Radar module withdrawal rails
11 AN/ALQ-165 transmitting antenna
12 Electro-luminescent formation lighting strip
13 Hughes AN/APG-65 multi-mode radar equipment module
14 AN/ALR-67 receiving antenna
15 Ventral AN/ALQ-165 transmitting antenna
16 Radar beacon antenna
17 Pitot head, port and starboard
18 Angle of attack transmitter
19 Night identification spotlight (Finnish and Kuwaiti aircraft)
20 Cannon and ammunition drum hydraulic-drive motor
21 Cannon mounting
22 Refuelling probe actuator
23 Frameless windscreen panel
24 Instrument panel shroud
25 M61A-1 120mm six-barrel rotary cannon
26 Ammunition feed chute
27 Front pressure bulkhead
28 Rudder pedals
29 Control column, quadriplex fly-by-wire control system
30 Kaiser multi-function CRT head-down displays
31 Kaiser AN/AVQ-28 head-up display
32 Upward hinged cockpit canopy
33 Pilot's rear view mirrors
34 Boarding ladder, extended
35 Hydraulic retraction jack
36 Cleveland nose undercarriage leg strut
37 UHF/TACAN aerial
38 Liquid oxygen converter
39 Cabin pressure regulator
40 Ejection seat headrest
41 Martin-Baker SJU-5/6 ejection seat
42 Port side console panel
43 Port side console panel
44 Engine throttle levers
45 Cockpit floor level
46 Avionics equipment bay, port and starboard
47 Landing lamp
48 Catapult launch signal lights
49 Hydraulic steering control
50 Catapult launch strop
51 Twin nosewheel, forward retracting
52 Wing root leading-edge extension
53 Front avionics equipment bay
54 Liquid oxygen converter
55 Rear pressure bulkhead
56 Canopy hinge point
57 Rear avionics equipment bays, port and starboard

61 Structural space provision for second seat (F/A-18D)
62 Canopy actuator
63 Canopy lock actuator
64 Rear pressure bulkhead
65 Canopy hinge point
66 Rear avionics equipment bays, port and starboard

67 Fuselage centreline pylon
68 Leading-edge extension frame construction
69 Fuselage void fire suppression foam filler
70 Forward fuselage self-sealing bag-type fuel tanks; total internal capacity 1,700 US gal (6,435 litres)
71 Fuselage top longeron
72 AN/ALQ-165 transmitting antennae
73 Starboard wing root leading-edge extension
74 Graphite/epoxy dorsal access panels
75 Starboard dorsal access panels
76 Fin aerodynamic load alleviating strake
77 TACAN aerial
78 AN/ALR-67 receiving antenna
79 Fuel tank access panels
80 Forward aircraft lifting fitting
81 Air conditioning liquid cooling system heat Avionics exchanger
82 Air conditioning system ram air intake
83 Boundary layer spill duct
84 Port position light
85 Intake ramp bleed air holes
86 Port engine intake
87 Intake duct framing
88 Cooling air spill ducts
89 Boundary layer spill duct
90 Air conditioning plant
91 Air conditioning heat exchanger exhaust
92 Leading-edge flap hydraulic motor and drive shaft
93 Wing root bolted attachment joints
94 Gun bay purging air vents
95 Center-section self-sealing fuel tanks
96 Fuel bay deck
97 Engine bleed air duct to air conditioning system
98 UHF/IFF/Data Link antenna
99 Starboard wing root joint
100 Inboard stores pylon
101 Mk.82, 500lb (227kg) Snakeye retarded bombs
102 Multiple ejector rack
103 Outboard stores pylon
104 Starboard wing integral fuel tanks
105 Wing fold joint
106 Wing folded position
107 Flap rotary hinge actuator
108 Aileron drooping aileron
109 Graphite/epoxy wing skin panelling
110 Starboard navigation light
111 Missile launch rail
112 AIM-9L Sidewinder air-to-air missile
113 Electro-luminescent formation lights
114 Wingtip folded position
115 Starboard drooping aileron
116 Aileron hydraulic actuator
117 Wing fold hydraulic actuator

118 Flap vane
119 Port single-slotted flap, down position
120 Flap external hinge
121 Flap panel hydraulic actuator
122 Rear fuselage self-sealing fuel tank
123 Hydraulic reservoirs, port and starboard
124 Starboard engine bay
125 Fin root attachment joint
126 Fin vent intake
127 Tailfin multi-spar construction
128 Rudder hydraulic actuator
129 Radar warning system power amplifier

130 Graphite/epoxy fin skin panels
131 Leading-edge honeycomb core construction
132 Titanium leading edge
133 Glass fibre fin tip fairing
134 Tail position light
135 AN/ALR-67 receiving antenna
136 AN/ALQ-165 low-band transmitting antenna

137 Fuel jettison
138 Starboard rudder
139 Rudder honeycomb core construction
140 Airbrake, open
141 Airbrake, all-moving tailplane
142 Graphite/epoxy airbrake frame construction
143 Hydraulic jack
144 Airbrake housing
145 Formation lighting strip
146 Fuel venting air intake
147 Anti-collision beacon, port and starboard
148 Port fin tip fairing
149 AN/ALQ-165 high-band transmitting antenna
150 AN/ALR-67 receiving antenna
151 AN/ALQ-165 antenna
152 Fuel jettison
153 Port rudder
154 Tailplane mounting frame
155 Afterburner ducting
156 Engine bay venting air louvers
157 Afterburner nozzle actuators
158 Nozzle sealing flaps
159 Variable area afterburner nozzles
160 Port all-moving tailplane
161 Graphite/epoxy tailplane skin panelling

162 Honeycomb core construction
163 Deck arrestor hook, lowered
164 Deck arrestor hook, lowered
165 Hinge control arm
166 Tailplane hydraulic actuator
167 Fully automatic digital engine control unit

168 Engine fuel control system equipment
169 Formation lighting strip
170 General Electric F404-GE-400 afterburning low-bypass turbofan engine
171 Port fin root attachment
172 Main engine mounting
173 Engine compressor intake
174 Aft aircraft lifting fittings, port and starboard
175 Central Auxiliary Power Unit (APU)
176 Airframe mounted accessory equipment gear-

181 Flap vane honeycomb core construction
182 Wing fold hydraulic actuator
183 Port dropping aileron
184 Outer wing panel multi-spar construction
185 Wing fold hinge joint
186 Outboard leading-edge flap segment rotary actuator
187 Leading-edge flap honeycomb core construction
188 Port navigation light
189 Formation lighting strip
190 AIM-9L Sidewinder air-to-air missile
191 Kelvin Air Combat Maneuvering Instrumentation pod (ACMI)
192 LAU-10 4.5in (127mm) rocket launcher
193 LAU-3CA 19 x 2.75in (70mm) rocket pack
194 B61 free-fall tactical nuclear weapon
195 2.75in (70mm) folding-fin aircraft rocket (FFAR)
196 5in (127mm) FFAR
197 GBU-10E/B laser-guided Mk.84 2,000lb (907kg) bomb
198 Mk.83 low-drag general purpose bombs (LDGB)
199 Horizontal ejector rack
200 Outboard stores pylon
201 Pylon attachment hardpoint
202 Leading-edge flap aluminium skin panelling

203 Port wing integral fuel tank
204 Multi-spar wing panel construction
205 Inboard pylon attachment hard point
206 Leading-edge flap rotary actuator
207 Inboard stores pylon
208 ANALE-39 chaff/flare dispenser
209 330 US gal (1,250 litres) external fuel tank
210 Levered suspension axle beam
211 Axle swivelling linkage
212 Shock absorber strut
213 Cleveland main undercarriage leg strut
214 Main undercarriage leg pivot mounting
215 ANALE-39 chaff/flare dispenser
216 Ventral AN/ALR-67 antenna
217 Strike camera housing
218 Fuselage lateral stores station adaptor
219 Martin-Marietta AN/ASQ-173 Laser Spot Tracker/Strike Camera pod (LST/CAM)
220 Port fuselage pylon adaptor
221 Ford ANAAS-38 forward-looking infra-red pod (FLIR)
222 AGM-84 Harpoon air-to-surface anti-shipping missile
223 AGM-88 HARM, high speed anti-radiation missile
224 AIM-7F Sparrow III air-to-air missile
225 AIM-120 AMRAAM, advanced medium-range air-to-air missile

box, port and starboard
177 Fuselage flank stores, station, missile carriage
178 Port flap, down position
179 Honeycomb core trailing-edge construction
180 Flap rib construction

Left: The second-production Swiss Air Force F-18D was also the first aircraft to be assembled in Switzerland. This photo was set against stunning alpine scenery during its first test flight in October 1996. (Boeing)

Left: One of the Swiss F-18Ds refuels from an Armée de l'Air (French Air Force) Boeing KC-135FR Stratotanker. (©Swiss Air Force)

Below: This photo reveals the underside of a Swiss F-18C and gives a good view of the inside of the undercarriage bays. (Key – Steve Fletcher)

F/A-18E/F SUPER HORNET

Below: The first prototype F/A-18E was rolled out on September 18, 1995, wearing the badges of two Navy units. On the port fin were the markings used by VF-142 'Ghost Riders', an Atlantic Fleet Northrop Grumman F-14 Tomcat squadron that had only recently disestablished in April 1995. On the starboard side, it wore the badge of VFA-131, even though under current plans neither of these two units will receive the aircraft.
(McDonnell Douglas)

Bottom: Fred Madenwald lifts the first prototype F/A-18E off the runway at Lambert International Airport, St Louis, during its maiden flight on November 29, 1995.
(McDonnell Douglas)

McDonnell Douglas conducted studies to enhance the existing Hornet design during the late 1980s, and after considering several different versions eventually decided on a larger version of the existing Hornet. With the cancellation of the McDonnell Douglas/General Dynamics A-12 Avenger II on January 7, 1991, the Navy suddenly found itself without a suitable replacement for several ageing aircraft.

Grumman proposed several new versions of the now ageing F-14 Tomcat in a final attempt to keep the aircraft in production. Unfortunately, the Department of Defense had already decided that the Tomcat production would cease after the already cut-down order for the F-14D had ended. The politicians who supported Grumman tried lobbying their case for more Tomcats, but only made more enemies within the government and Department of Defense. The government increasingly looked to McDonnell Douglas to provide a new aircraft due to the reliability and proven versatility of the existing Hornet and the lower cost of the proposed aircraft. The Navy soon chose the improved version of the F-18, and McDonnell Douglas was awarded a formal development contract to produce five F/A-18Es, two F/A-18Fs and three non-flying static test airframes on December 7, 1992.

Although the aircraft is essentially a larger version of the Hornet, it has little in common with the previous aircraft apart from some avionics similar to late-production F/A-18C/D airframes and the APG-73 radar. Among the many changes is the F414 engine, which was developed from an upgraded version of the F404 used to power the A-12, although the new engine is not inter-changeable with an earlier F404. The first prototype Super Hornet, F/A-18E (165164), was named the Super Hornet during its roll-out ceremony at St Louis on September 18, 1995. It was on schedule, within budget and 1,000lb (454kg) under its specification weight. The first F/A-18E made its first flight on November 29, 1995, with the second aircraft following it into the air on December 26. They flew to Patuxent River in February 1996 to commence flight tests. The first F/A-18F (165166) flew on April 1, with the remaining aircraft following over the next eight months and the last aircraft F/A-18E (165167) making its first flight on January 2, 1997.

The test programme intensified, with the aircraft making its first carrier landing aboard USS *John C Stennis* in January 1997 and the last test aircraft being delivered to Patuxent River on February 1, 1997. During the 1997 Quadrennial Defense Review, the original order was cut

Left: A close-up of the Super Hornet's cockpit, which is essentially the same as late-production F/A-18C/D cockpit, though notable differences include the touch-button up-front control display screen in the centre, and the new engine control panel on the lower left next to the moving map. (McDonnell Douglas)

Below: One of the most colourful paint schemes worn is the high-visibility red and white scheme applied to the fourth prototype. This aircraft was originally used for high angle of attack trials, and the colours were added for the ground-tracking cameras. (McDonnell Douglas)

Bottom: Up to 59 different weapons combinations were tried during separation trials on the Super Hornet and all of these were due to have been cleared ready for the first fleet deployment. Here, the first F/A-18E is carrying two AGM-154 JSOWs, two AGM-65 Mavericks and a pair of AIM-7 Sparrows. (Boeing)

45

Left: Equipped with cameras and wearing photographic calibration markings, the second prototype is carrying four AIM-120 AMRAAMs during live firing trials of the missile. (Boeing)

Below: One of the roles the Super Hornet will take on is the buddy tanker role currently performed by the Lockheed Martin S-3B Viking. (USN – Kurt Langfield)

Bottom: The final pre-Operational Evaluation carrier qualification trials were performed aboard USS *Harry S Truman* off the coast of Florida in February and March 1999. (Boeing)

Right: The first-production F/A-18E, complete in the markings of VX-9, enters the circuit pattern prior to landing at NAS Patuxent River. (Boeing)

Below and bottom: Two of the Super Hornets assigned to the Weapons Test Squadron at NAWS China Lake. The fourth-production F/A-18E is fitted with an AN/ALE-50 Towed Decoy System (TDS). The F/A-18F is fitted with the Raytheon ASQ-228 ATFLIR pod.(Both USN via Jim Winchester)

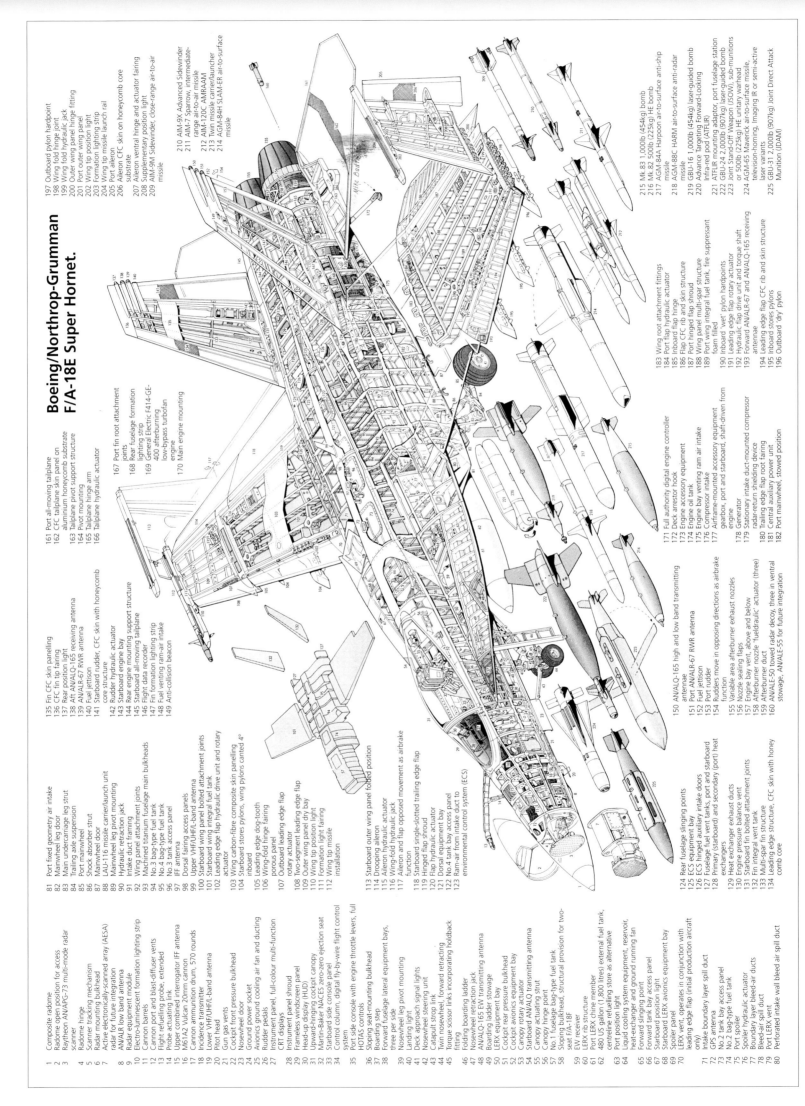

Boeing/Northrop-Grumman F/A-18E Super Hornet.

1 Composite radome
2 Radome open position for access
3 Raytheon AN/APG-73 multi-mode radar scanner
4 Radome hinge
5 Scanner tracking mechanism
6 Radar mounting bulkhead
7 Active electronically-scanned array (AESA) radar for future integration
8 AN/ALR low band antenna
9 Radar equipment module
10 Electro-luminescent formation lighting strip
11 Cannon barrels
12 Cannon port and blast-diffuser vents
13 Incidence transmitter
14 Flight refuelling probe, extended
15 Upper combined interrogator IFF antenna
16 M61A2 Vulcan 20mm cannon
17 Cannon ammunition drum, 570 rounds
18 Lower VHF/UHF/L-band antenna
19 Pitot head
20 Pitot head
21 Gun gas vents
22 Cockpit front pressure bulkhead
23 Nosewheel door
24 Ground power socket
25 Avionics ground cooling air fan and ducting
26 Rudder pedals
27 Instrument panel, full-colour multi-function CRT displays
28 Instrument panel shroud
29 Frameless windscreen panel
30 Head-up display (HUD)
31 Upward-hinging canopy
32 Martin-Baker NACES zero-zero ejection seat
33 Starboard side console panels
34 Control column, digital fly-by-wire flight control system
35 Port side console with engine throttle levers, full HOTAS controls
36 Sloping seat-mounting bulkhead
37 Boarding step
38 Forward fuselage lateral equipment bays, three per side
39 Nosewheel leg pivot mounting
40 Landing light
41 Deck approach signal lights
42 GPS antenna
43 Catapult strop link
44 Twin nosewheel, forward retracting
45 Torque scissor links incorporating holdback fitting
46 Folding boarding ladder
47 Nosewheel retraction jack
48 AN/ALQ-165 EW transmitting antenna
49 Boarding ladder stowage
50 LERX equipment bay
51 Cockpit rear pressure bulkhead
52 Cockpit avionics equipment bay
53 Canopy rotary actuator
54 Starboard AN/ALQ transmitting antenna
55 Canopy actuating strut
56 Canopy hinge point
57 No.1 fuselage bag-type fuel tank
58 Sloping bulkhead, structural provision for two-seat F/A-18F
59 EW receiver
60 LERX receiver
61 Port LERX chine member
62 480 US gallon (1,800 litres) external fuel tank, centreline refuelling store as alternative
63 Port position light
64 Liquid cooling system equipment, reservoir, heat-exchanger and ground running fan
65 Forward slinging point
66 Forward tank bay access panel
67 Starboard position light
68 Starboard LERX avionics equipment bay
69 Spoiler panel
70 Leading edge flap (initial production aircraft only)
71 Intake boundary layer spill duct
72 No.2 tank bay access panel
73 No.2 bag-type fuel tank
74 No.2 bag-type fuel tank
75 Port spoiler
76 Spoiler hydraulic actuator
77 Boundary layer bleed-air ducts
78 Bleed-air spill duct
79 Port LERX vent
80 Perforated intake wall bleed air spill duct

81 Port fixed geometry air intake
82 Mainwheel leg pivot
83 Main undercarriage leg strut
84 Trailing axle suspension
85 Port mainwheel
86 Shock absorber strut
87 Mainwheel door
88 LAU-116 missile carrier/launch unit
89 Mainwheel leg pivot mounting
90 Hydraulic retraction jack
91 Intake duct framing
92 Wing panel attachment joints
93 Machined titanium fuselage main bulkheads
94 No.3 bag-type fuel tank
95 No.4 bag-type fuel tank
96 No.3 tank access panel
97 IFF antenna
98 Dorsal fairing access panels
99 Upper VHF/UHF/L-band antenna
100 Starboard wing panel bolted attachment joints
101 Starboard wing integral fuel tank
102 Leading edge flap hydraulic drive unit and rotary actuator
103 Wing carbon-fibre composite skin panelling
104 Starboard stores pylons, wing pylons canted 4° inboard
105 Leading edge dog-tooth
106 Wing-fold hinge fairing
107 Outboard leading edge flap porous panel
108 Two-segment leading edge flap
109 Outer wing panel dry bay
110 Wing tip position light
111 Formation light fairing
112 Wing tip missile installation
113 Starboard outer wing panel folded position
114 Drooping aileron
115 Aileron hydraulic actuator
116 Wing-fold hydraulic jack
117 Aileron and flap opposed movement as airbrake function
118 Starboard single-slotted trailing edge flap
119 Hinged flap shroud
120 Flap hydraulic actuator
121 Dorsal equipment bay
122 No.4 tank bay access panel
123 Ram-air from intake duct to environmental control system (ECS)
124 Rear fuselage slinging points
125 ECS equipment bay
126 ECS hinged auxiliary intake doors
127 Fuselage fuel vent tanks, port and starboard
128 Primary (starboard) and secondary (port) heat exchangers
129 Heat exchanger exhaust ducts
130 Engine pressure balance vent
131 Starboard fin bolted attachment joints
132 Fin integral vent tank
133 Multi-spar fin structure
134 Leading edge structure, CFC skin with honey comb core

135 Fin CFC skin panelling
136 CFC fin tip fairing
137 Rear position light
138 Aft AN/ALQ-165 receiving antenna
139 AN/ALR-67 RWR antenna
140 Fuel jettison
141 Starboard rudder, CFC skin with honeycomb core structure
142 Rudder hydraulic actuator
143 Starboard engine bay
144 Rear engine mounting tailplane support structure
145 Starboard all-moving tailplane
146 Flight data recorder
147 Fin formation lighting strip
148 Fuel venting ram-air intake
149 Anti-collision beacon
150 AN/ALQ-165 high and low band transmitting antennae
151 Port AN/ALR-67 RWR antenna
152 Fuel jettison
153 Port rudder
154 Rudders move in opposing directions as airbrake function
155 Variable area afterburner exhaust nozzles
156 Nozzle sealing flaps
157 Engine bay vent, above and below
158 Afterburner nozzle 'fueldraulic' actuator (three)
159 Afterburner duct
160 AN/ALE-50 towed radar decoy, three in ventral stowage, AN/ALE-55 for future integration

161 Port all-moving tailplane
162 CFC tailplane skin panel on aluminium honeycomb substrate
163 Tailplane pivot support structure
164 Pivot mounting
165 Tailplane hinge arm
166 Tailplane hydraulic actuator
167 Port fin root attachment joints
168 Rear fuselage formation lighting strip
169 General Electric F414-GE-400 afterburning low-bypass turbofan engine
170 Main engine mounting

171 Full authority digital engine controller
172 Deck arrestor hook
173 Engine accessory equipment
174 Engine oil tank
175 Engine bay venting ram-air intake
176 Compressor intake
177 Airframe-mounted accessory equipment gearbox, port and starboard, shaft-driven from engine
178 Generator
179 Stationary intake duct-mounted compressor radar-return shielding device
180 Trailing edge flap root fairing
181 Central auxiliary power unit
182 Port mainwheel, stowed position
183 Wing root attachment fittings
184 Port flap hydraulic actuator
185 Inboard flap hinge
186 Flap CFC rib and skin structure
187 Port hinged flap shroud
188 Wing panel multi-spar structure
189 Port wing integral fuel tank, fire suppressant foam filled
190 Inboard 'wet' pylon hardpoints
191 Leading edge flap rotary actuator
192 Hydraulic flap drive unit and torque shaft
193 Forward AN/ALR-67 and AN/ALQ-165 receiving antennae
194 Leading edge flap CFC rib and skin structure
195 Inboard stores pylons
196 Outboard 'dry' pylon

197 Outboard pylon hardpoint
198 Wing fold hinge joint
199 Wing fold hydraulic jack
200 Outer wing panel hinge fitting
201 Port outer wing panel
202 Wing tip position light
203 Formation lighting strip
204 Wing tip missile launch rail
205 Port aileron
206 Aileron CFC skin on honeycomb core substrate
207 Aileron ventral hinge and actuator fairing
208 Supplementary position light
209 AIM-9M Sidewinder, close-range air-to-air missile
210 AIM-9X Advanced Sidewinder
211 AIM-7 Sparrow, intermediate-range air-to-air missile
212 AIM-120C AMRAAM
213 Twin missile carrier/launcher
214 AGM-84H SLAM-ER air-to-surface missile
215 Mk 83 1,000lb (454kg) bomb
216 Mk 82 500lb (225kg) HE bomb
217 AGM-84A Harpoon air-to-surface anti-ship missile
218 AGM-88C HARM air-to-surface anti-radar missile
219 GBU-16 1,000lb (454kg) laser-guided bomb
220 Advance Targeting Forward-Looking Infra-red pod (ATFLIR)
221 ATFLIR mounting adaptor, port fuselage station
222 GBU-24 2,000lb (907kg) laser-guided bomb
223 Joint Stand-Off Weapon (JSOW), sub-munitions or 500lb (225kg) HE unitary warhead
224 AGM-65 Maverick air-to-surface, television-homing, Imaging IR or semi-active laser variants
225 GBU-31 2,000lb (907kg) Joint Direct Attack Munition (JDAM)

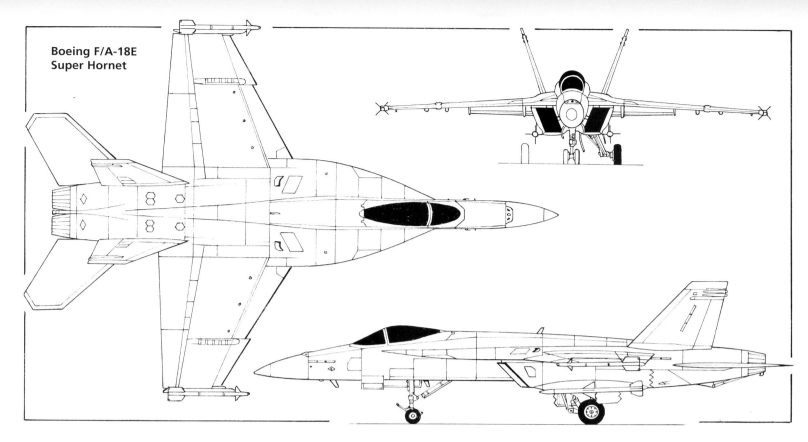

**Boeing F/A-18E
Super Hornet**

Below: This drawing to the same scale illustrates the difference in size and layout between the two aircraft an F/A-18C and an F/A-18E.

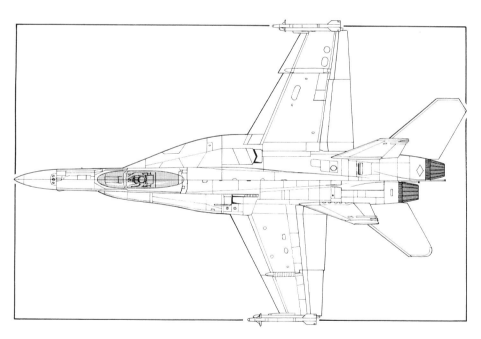

F/A-18E SPECIFICATION DATA

Length overall:	60ft 3½in (18.38m)
Wingspan over missiles:	44ft 8½in (13.62m)
Width, wings folded:	32ft 7¼in (9.94m)
Height:	16ft 0in (4.88m)
Tailplane span:	21ft 7¾in (6.58m)
Empty weight:	30,564lb (13,864kg)
Maximum internal fuel:	14,460lb (6,559kg)
External fuel:	16,380lb (7,430kg)
Maximum external stores load:	17,700lb (7,710kg)
Maximum level speed:	More than Mach 1.8
Maximum level speed, intermediate power:	More than Mach 1.0
Approach speed:	125 knots (232km/h 144mph)
Powerplant:	Two General Electric F414-GE-400s, each producing 22,000lb (97.9kN) thrust

from 1,000 aircraft down to the current 548 requirement, although it was made clear that this depended on the development and progress of the Joint Strike Fighter (JSF) programme.

The first-production F/A-18E (165533) made its first flight on November 6, 1998, while the follow-on sea trials aboard USS *Harry S Truman* were performed by the second prototype in March 1999. The first three production batches were purchased as Low Rate Initial Production (LRIP) aircraft, with the first of these going to VX-9, which ran the Operational Evaluation (OPEVAL) from May 1999 through to November that year. The last of the 12 LRIP 1 aircraft was delivered two months ahead of schedule to Patuxent River on November 9, 1999. The first Fleet Replacement Squadron (FRS) VFA-122, a former A-7 FRS, was re-established at Lemoore NAS on January 15, 1999, although it did not actually receive its first seven aircraft until November 18.

The second prototype notched up a milestone on December 13, 1999, when it flew the test fleet's 5,000th flying hour. Meanwhile, deliveries of the 20 LRIP 2s and 30 LRIP 3s continued apace. VFA-122 finally started training Instructors, Weapons Systems Operators (WSO) and maintenance personnel before commencing individual unit conversion training in June 2000, at the same time as a full-rate production contract for 222 airframes was signed on June 15. The Super Hornet will eventually replace the Northrop Grumman F-14 Tomcat, and several squadrons of F/A-18Cs within the Navy. The first active fleet unit to be declared operational with the F/A-18E was VFA-115, which had previously flown the F/A-18C and which received its first aircraft on December 7, 2000. The next two squadrons to convert to the Super Hornet were VF-14 and VF-41. Unlike VFA-115, these units had both converted from the Northrop Grumman F-14 Tomcat and both had just completed an extended last cruise aboard USS *Enterprise* as part of Operation Enduring Freedom.

On return to Oceana NAS Virginia, they disestablished and reformed at Lemoore, California, shortly after

in December 2001. Both units have changed their designations to reflect their multi-role operations. VFA-14 now operates the F/A-18E, while VFA-41 converted to the F/A-18F. Once they have declared combat-ready, they joined CVW-11 aboard USS *Nimitz* for a WestPac cruise in 2003. VF-102 commenced conversion to the F/A-18F at the end of May 2002, current plans released at the beginning of 2003 meant that all the remaining F-14 squadrons, together with several F/A-18C units, were due to have completed their conversion to the new aircraft by 2008.

Another role the Super Hornet will take on is that of dedicated tanker, as the US Navy has not had a dedicated tanker aircraft since the retirement of the Grumman KA-6D Intruder in 1996. This role is currently performed by the Lockheed Martin S-3B Viking, even more so as it has relinquished its anti-submarine role to land-based Lockheed Martin P-3 Orions and ship-based Sikorsky SH-60B/Fs Seahawks. At the moment, the Super Hornet is fitted with the standard Hornet radar, but it will eventually be fitted with the new AN/APG-79 Active Electronically Steered Array (AESA) that is currently undergoing development, with flight testing due to commence in 2003.

Under plans announced in 2002 to implement more integration between Marine and Navy Carrier Air Wings, further cuts to the Super Hornet production run could be implemented, though this depends on the outcome of the service trials of the Lockheed F-35 JSF. The production of

the Super Hornet could be extended if the Marines and Navy chose the F/A-18 Command and Control Warfare (C2W) variant. This programme began as a private venture when the Navy awarded a small contract to McDonnell Douglas to study the possibility of converting an F/A-18F into an electronic warfare platform to replace the Grumman EA-6B Prowler. McDonnell Douglas teamed up with Northrop Grumman in 1996 for systems integration work due to Northrop having produced the EA-6 and the systems that were incorporated into the EF-111 Raven.

When funding for the Navy study ended, both companies continued funding the project themselves. As the studies progressed, the aircraft gained several different names, including the Airborne Electronic Attack (AEA) variant, the F/A-18G 'Growler' and more recently the EA-18G. If the aircraft is chosen, an additional 100-plus aircraft could be ordered. Although the Marines seem to prefer an electronic attack version of the Lockheed F-35 JSF, they might choose the EA-18 as an interim measure as the F-35 is unlikely to enter service before 2010.

Boeing commenced negotiations with the first potential export customer, Malaysia, in September 2002 after it expressed an interest in purchasing up to 18 F/A-18Fs, and 36 General Electric F414 engines, with three spare engines. If the deal is successful, it could also include exchanging the eight F/A-18Ds currently in service as part of the purchase.

Above: A four-ship of Super Hornets over the Californian desert. The two nearest aircraft, both F/A-18Es, belong to the Pacific Fleet FRS VFA-122, while the two leading aircraft are from VX-9. (Boeing)

Bottom right: Photographed while the unit was working up to operational readiness with the F/A-18E in October 2002, VFA-14 was one of the first Navy units to convert from the F-14 Tomcat. The Navy currently plans to retire all three versions of the Tomcat by 2007, with all the units intended to convert to the Super Hornet to be completed by 2008. (USN -PM3 Inez Lawson)

Right: Prior to operating the F/A-18E, VFA-115 flew the F/A-18C within Carrier Air Wing 14. The squadron was a junior unit within the Hornet community, having converted from the Grumman A-6E Intruder in 1996. One of the squadron's aircraft departs from USS *Abraham Lincoln* in October 2002, carrying a pair of GBU-32 JDAMs, while the unit was undertaking the first operational deployment of the Super Hornet. At the same time, it also deployed the new Raytheon ASQ-228 Advanced Tactical Forward-Looking Infra-Red (ATFLIR) pod. The pod has improved targeting performance both in the EO and IR imagery modes, and boasts three to five times' better maintainability. It will eventually replace the earlier AAS-38 Nite Hawk pod throughout the Navy and possibly the Marine Hornet fleet. (USN – PMA Philip A McDaniel)

Right: VFA-41 the 'Black Aces' joined VFA-14 at Lemoore to begin conversion to the F/A-18F, after flying the F-14 as an Atlantic Fleet unit for almost 26 years. While flying Tomcats, they achieved the first kills for the aircraft when they shot down two Libyan Air Force Sukhoi Su-22 Fitters on August 19, 1981. The small star marking at the base of the fin is the Carrier Air Wing 11 badge. (USN – PM3 Inez Lawson)

Opposite page, top: The first aircraft for VFA-102 started to appear when the unit commenced conversion in early 2002. One of the unit's aircraft participated at the Farnborough air show in July, when it accompanied an aircraft from VFA-41. One of the unit's aircraft is seen preparing to launch from the USS *John C Stennis* during February 2003. (USN - PM3 Joshua Word)

Opposite page, bottom: Boeing has proposed as many as 180 E/A-18G airframes, although this may be reduced to 90 airframes depending on USAF and USMC interest in the programme. The six-year Future Years Defense Program, which the Department of Defense submitted to Congress on

February 3, 2003, included reducing Super Hornet production from the original 50 aircraft per year to 46 in FY03. This would then be reduced to 42 per year in both FY04 and FY05, which would enable funding of the E/A-18G to commence in 2005, with the first four aircraft of a order for 78 due to be funded in 2006. (Boeing)

Above: The first prototype F/A-18F performed an initial flight demonstration of the EA-18 concept in November 2001. The aircraft is fitted with three ALQ-99 jamming pods borrowed from the EA-6B community. (Boeing)

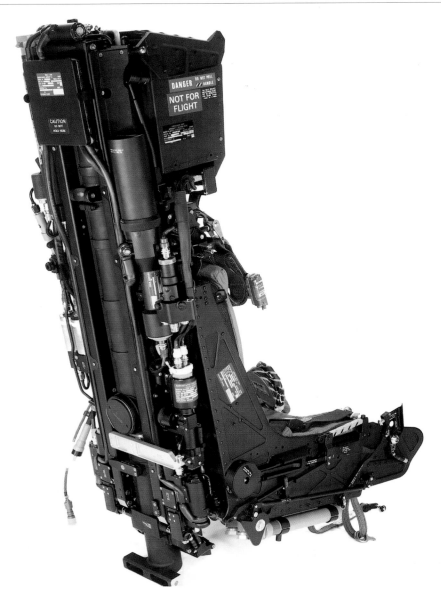

Above: This photo illustrates the excellent all-round visibility from the cockpit on this Swiss Air Force F-18C. Canadian, Finnish, Kuwaiti and Swiss examples are all fitted with the night identification light mounted in the nose panel, which is also used as the access panel to the M61 cannon ammunition bay. (Key – Steve Fletcher)

Right and below: All F/A-18s are equipped with Martin-Baker ejection seats and all carry the following US designations: early model aircraft have the SJU-6/A fitted in the front and two-seaters have an SJU-5/A in the rear; later airframes have SJU-17-1/A in the front and SJU-17-2/A in the rear. (Martin-Baker)

Above: The F/A-18 Super Hornet has two prominent antennae on the forward fuselage. Just in front of the canopy windscreen is the APX-111 Combined Interrogator Transponder (CIT). The Angle of Attack (AoA) vane is attached to the side of the nose and surrounding this is a diamond-shape section that helps reduce the radar cross-section of the aircraft. (Key -Mark Nicholls)

Left: Most early-production Hornets were fitted with the Raytheon (formerly Hughes) AN/APG-65 radar, while all late-production aircraft have been fitted with the AN/APG-73 illustrated here. Some of the early-production C/D models have had this refitted, while the surplus AN/APG-65 have been passed back to Boeing for use in the AV-8B+ conversion programme. The radar has been pulled forward on built-in rails for maintenance – the cannon ports are also visible in this view. (Hughes)

Left: Australian F/A-18s are not fitted with the carrier approach attitude indicator, while several also appear to have had the catapult launch bar removed. However, they have two landing lights fitted to the main part of the nosewheel.

Below: The twin-nose-wheel undercarriage leg is steered using a combination of a switch on the control stick and through inputs to the rudder pedals. The wheel can be turned through 75° for slow speed taxying and 16° for taxying at higher speeds. The carrier approach attitude indicators are fitted into the small box at the top of the leg, and have three small indicator lights inside. (Key – Mark Nicholls)

Below: Although the first production Super Hornets are fitted with the AN/APG-73, new-build aircraft will eventually receive the new Raytheon AN/APG-79 Active Electronically Scanned Array (AESA) radar that will commence flight testing in 2003. (Raytheon)

Above: As with all carrier-borne aircraft, the Hornet's undercarriage is very robust and can withstand the immense impacts that come from constantly hitting carrier decks. The main gear retract backwards through 90° to lie flat against the bottom of the air intake ducts. (Key – Mark Nicholls)

Above: While all first-generation Hornets have straight main undercarriage well doors, these were redesigned for the Super Hornet and use stealthy 'faceted' or jagged edges, to deflect radar emissions (Key – Mark Nicholls)

Below: First-generation Hornets have a simple D-shape air intake that is partially visible in this photograph taken aboard USS *John C Stennis* in February 2002. (Key -Dave Willis)

Bottom: One modification added to the F/A-18 after it entered service was the attachment of small fences to both LEXs. They were added after buffeting caused by air flow around the LEXs resulted in fatigue cracks in the fin and fuselage joints. (Key -Dave Willis)

Above: Tie-down attachments fitted on the airframe enable groundcrew to perform routine maintenance on deck without fear of sudden movement by the aircraft. This F/A-18C from VFA-147 is securely chained to USS *Nimitz* during a visit to Hong Kong in 1993. (Key -Duncan Cubitt)

Below: One of the more novel features fitted to the Hornet is the retractable crew access ladder that manually retracts into a well on the port wing leading-edge extension. (Key -Dave Willis)

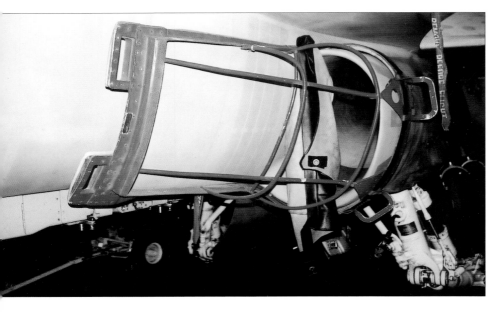

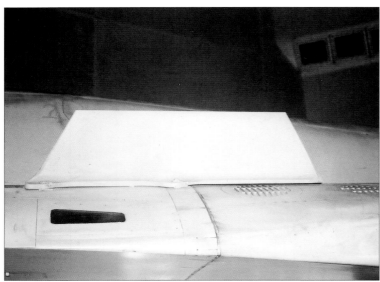

Above: Super Hornets have gained an extra weapons pylon under both wings, which gives increased weapons-carrying ability over the standard Hornet. This F/A-18F from VFA-41 is carrying Multiple Ejector Racks (MER), which are used specifically for carriage of up to six practice bombs. (Key -Mark Nicholls)

Above: When the YF-17 design was revised and gradually became the Hornet, it gained a folding wing so that it could fit in the tight confines of carrier flight deck and hangars. (Key -Dave Willis)

Left: This view of USS *America's* hangar deck taken in 1989 gives some idea of how much maintenance work is often carried out while a squadron is deployed. The Hornet in the foreground is undergoing remedial work to its paint scheme. (Key -Duncan Cubitt)

Left: Marine Corps Hornet displaying at Farnborough in 1996. This underside view shows the undercarriage arrangement and, with the absence of pylon and stores, the overall aerodynamic lines of the F-18. (Key -Duncan Cubitt)

Below: All versions of the Hornet family have wingtip pylons for carriage of AIM-9 Sidewinder or AIM-132 ASRAAM missiles. The pylons can also be used to carry instrumented pods for use during air combat training, as well as specially-modified cameras for use in weapons separation tests. (Key – Mark Nicholls)

Below right: Electro-luminescent lighting strips have been fitted to all versions of the Hornet family – these are fitted on the nose tail and fuselage, as illustrated here. (Key – Dave Willis)

Bottom: All models of the Hornet have provision for several Electronic Counter Measures (ECM) antennae to be fitted to the rear of the fin. The Sanders, now Lockheed Martin ALQ-126B, is fitted to all F/A-18A and 'B models, as illustrated on this Spanish EF-18A. (Key Steve Fletcher)

Bottom middle: With the introduction of the F/A-18C and 'D into service, the US Navy planned to replace the ALQ-126 with the AN/ALQ-165 Airborne Self Protection Jammer (ASPJ). However, this was halted after only 96 kits had been delivered, and these were initially issued when the aircraft were operating in high-threat environments. All export Hornets are fitted with this system as standard, while the US Navy has subsequently received several more batches. This brightly-coloured F/A-18C is from VMFA-232, based at MCAS Miramar, California. (Key – Dave Allport)

Bottom right: This view of an F/A-18F from VFA-41 illustrates the enlarged tailplane fitted to the Super Hornet. (Key – Mark Nicholls)

Top left: All Hornets are equipped with an in-flight refuelling probe and can receive fuel from several types of tanker aircraft. Although the USAF use the 'Flying Boom' system, this can be overcome by attaching a drogue basket to the end of the boom on USAF KC-10 and KC-135 aircraft or by using the wingtip-mounted pods that have been fitted to both these types. (Boeing)

Above: Ground refuelling of the F/A-18 is achieved via the single-point receptacle seen here on these F/A-18Cs from VFA-25. (US Department of Defense)

Upper left: One of the General Electric F404-GE-402 engines has been removed from this F/A-18C for maintenance, giving a good view of the engine bay. The removal of the engine cover also makes it easier to see the arrestor hook fitted to the Hornet family. (Key – Dave Willis)

Left: While US Navy aircraft carriers are deployed at sea, they do not have access to some of the more usual facilities found ashore. This F404 engine is being tested on the new Jet Engine Test Instrumentation (JETI) system installed aboard USS *Nimitz* in 2002. (USN – PHAN Sara Bohannan)

Below: The proven General Electric F404 was used as the basis for the new F414-GE-400 engine for the Super Hornet. However, it includes technology used in the design of the F412 engine that would have powered the Boeing/McDonnell Douglas A-12 Avenger that was cancelled in 1991. (General Electric)

Left: An AIM-9 Sidewinder caught seconds after being fired from the first production Swiss F-18C, during the first phase of weapons verification testing for the Swiss Air Force. Interestingly, the aircraft has its night-time identification light switched on possibly for tracking purposes. (Boeing)

Left: The newest model of the Sidewinder family is the AIM-9X, due for a planned service entry date of 2003. One of them is seen mounted on the starboard wingtip pylon of an F/A-18F from VFA-122. (Key – Duncan Cubitt)

Left: This F/A-18A from VMFA-323 is seen in 1986 firing an AIM-7 Sparrow. The Sparrow is still in service with the US Navy, and can frequently be seen carried on both the Hornet and Super Hornet. Although it has largely been replaced by the AMRAAM, production of the Sparrow continues, with the AIM-7R being the current version, while older models are being upgraded to AIM-7P standard. (McDonnell Douglas)

Left: Initial test firing of AIM-9X missiles was conducted during 1999 and 2000 by Navy F/A-18Cs and Air Force Boeing F-15Cs. (Raytheon)

Right: A close-up view of the most recent version of the AMRAAM, the AIM-120C, seen during trials at the Naval Air Warfare Center at NAS Point Mugu, California. (USN – Vance Vasquez)

Right: The second proto-type F/A-18F was the first Super Hornet to fire an AIM-120 during the weapons certification pro-gramme. (USN – Vernon Pugh)

Below: Australia has become the first export customer for the AIM-132 ASRAAM, which is built by a consortium of European companies comprising Matra, BAE Dynamics, Aérospatiale Matra Missiles and Alenia Marconi Systems, which merged to form MBDA in April 2001. ASRAAM has been chosen as part of the Hornet upgrade. (MBDA)

Bottom left: An F/A-18C of VFA-22 carrying the AGM-62 Walleye which was developed during the 1960s as a low-cost TV-guided stand-off missile based on both Mk.83 and Mk.84 LDGP bombs. Whenever a Hornet carries a Walleye, it also carries a datalink pod to transfer data to and from the weapon when it has been fired. The US Navy is gradually replacing Walleye with the SLAM and SLAM-ER. (McDonnell Douglas)

Below: This sequence of photographs was taken during test firing of an IR (Infra-red)-guided AGM-65F Maverick from an F/A-18D flying at 10,000ft (3,048m) over the Pacific in July 1990. The target on this occasion was a small boat. (Hughes)

Right: A pair of F/A-18Cs from VFA-82 captured on camera during a training flight – the aircraft in the foreground is carrying drill rounds for the AGM-84 Harpoon anti-ship missile. (McDonnell Douglas)

Right: The AGM-84 served as the basis for the modified AGM-84E Stand-off Land Attack Missile (SLAM). The process involved replacing the Harpoon's active seeker head with an Imaging Infra-Red (IIR) seeker from the AGM-65D, together with a GPS receiver and a datalink. SLAM entered service in 1990 and was used successfully during Operation Desert Storm while undergoing operational evaluation. (McDonnell Douglas)

Lower right: Successful trials with the SLAM led to an improved version, the AGM-84H SLAM-ER (Expanded Response), an even more capable version, although it is shorter and is used exclusively by US Navy F/A-18 squadrons. (McDonnell Douglas)

Bottom: This early-production F/A-18A is seen firing off an AGM-88 HARM during missile trials. The aircraft is also carrying a more potent weapon on the starboard (right) wing in the form of a B61 tactical nuclear device, one of the few weapons that Hornets have ever had to use in anger.

Above left: SLAM-ER has now been cleared for carriage on both late-model F/A-18C/D and the Super Hornet, and has been used operationally in Afghanistan and Iraq. Some 700 earlier SLAMs will undergo an upgrade to SLAM-ER configuration. (Boeing)

Above right: Trials on an upgraded version of the AGM-88 for the US Navy, currently known as the Advanced Anti-Radiation Missile (AARGM), took place in August 2001, when the Weapons Test Squadron at NAS China Lake fired one of the pair carried on this F/A-18D. The missile successfully identified, tracked and guided itself to a simulated air defence radar target and destroyed it. (US Navy)

Right: A weapon that is rarely seen, except when it has been removed to undergo maintenance, is the M61 cannon fitted in the nose section above and behind the radar bay. Some late-model Hornets have been fitted with a new lighter version known as the M61-A2, which is also installed in the Super Hornet. (US Navy – Amy DelaTorres)

Below: A standard Mk.84 2,000lb (907kg) LDGP is seen here being dropped by an F/A-18D from VMFA (AW)-533. (McDonnell Douglas)

Below: An early-production F/A-18A from VFA-113, seen while dropping two 1,000lb (447kg) Mk.83 Low-Drag General Purpose Bombs (LDGP) now used exclusively by the US Navy and US Marine Corps. (McDonnell Douglas)

Left: With the addition of a Global Positioning System (GPS)-aided inertial guidance kit fitted into a modified tail assembly, the Mk.84 LDGP bomb becomes a Glide Bomb Unit (GBU)-32 JDAM. The orange bracing plates fitted to the bomb itself are designed to improve airflow around the bomb after it has been released. (Boeing)

Below left: The US Navy first used the AGM-154 Joint Stand-Off Weapon (JSOW) operationally in January 1999, when it was used to attack several targets in Iraq during Operation Southern Watch. This F/A-18C from the Naval Weapons Test Center was photographed carrying two AGM-154s, while engaged on separation trials. However, the standard number of JSOWs carried on operational missions would subsequently be increased to four. (US Navy)

Bottom left: The AN/AAS-38 LTD/R is gradually replacing its predecessor, the Lockheed Martin AN/ASQ-173 Laser Spot Tracker/Camera (LST/CAM), although the pod – based on the Pave Penny pod carried on USAF Fairchild A-10 Thunderbolt IIs – is still carried on numerous occasions. (Key – Alan Warnes)

Bottom right: As a result of tragic accidents during the Vietnam conflict, all LDGP and laser-guided bombs aboard aircraft carriers have a thermal coating to protect them from heat and prevent them 'cooking off' in the event of any mishap aboard a carrier. This coating, which is usually grey, gives the bomb a slightly rough appearance – it can be seen here applied to this GBU-16 Mk.83. (Key – Alan Warnes)

Left: Although the first AN/AAS-38 NITE Hawk FLIR pod was delivered to the US Navy in December 1983, the first Laser Target Designator/Ranger (LTD/R) version was not delivered until early 1993. The pod can be seen mounted on the port (left) side of the fuselage next to the GBU-16, seen here under the wing of this VFA-137 F/A-18C. (Boeing)

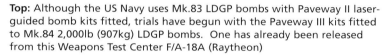

Top: Although the US Navy uses Mk.83 LDGP bombs with Paveway II laser-guided bomb kits fitted, trials have begun with the Paveway III kits fitted to Mk.84 2,000lb (907kg) LDGP bombs. One has already been released from this Weapons Test Center F/A-18A (Raytheon)

Above: Australian and Canadian Hornets often carry the more capable Canadian Rocket Vehicle (CRV)-7, which is a highly accurate 2.75in (70mm) unguided rocket originally designed by the Department of National Defence (DND) and Bristol Aerospace. (DND)

Right: US Navy and Marine Corps Hornets also use unguided rockets, although they are mainly used in the Forward Air Control-Airborne (FACA) role to mark targets. These VFA-147 F/A-18Cs are firing 5in (125mm) Zunis during a training exercise in 1990. (McDonnell Douglas)

Right: The fifth prototype Super Hornet captured dropping seven Mk.20 Rockeye cluster bombs during weapons release trials. (Boeing)

Below: Once integration and service trials are completed, both versions of the Super Hornet will carry the new SHAred Reconnaissance Pod (SHARP) which entered operational service with VFA-41 aboard USS *Nimitz* in 2003. Earlier Hornets will also be able to carry the pod, which is equipped with numerous advanced sensors and is carried on the centreline stores station. The second prototype F/A-18F is seen flying over the Pentagon during trials in August 2001. (US Navy)

8 F/A-18 OPERATORS

RAAF F/A-18 Hornet

2 Operational
Conversion Unit

3 Squadron

The list of operators presented here includes all the countries, wings and squadrons flying the F/A-18. Squadron nicknames have been included where they are known. Also included are complete serial allocations and aircraft write-offs, along with dates and serials where known. Air Forces Monthly the UK monthly published magazine regularly features updates on unit changes and aircraft losses.

AUSTRALIA	
Royal Australian Air Force	
3 Squadron	RAAF Williamtown
75 Squadron	RAAF Tindal
77 Squadron	RAAF Williamtown
2 Operational Conversion Unit (OCU)	RAAF Williamtown
Aircraft Research and Development Unit (ARDU)	RAAF Edinburgh

F/A-18A	**F/A-18B**
A21-1 to A21-57	A21-101 to A21-118

Losses	
A21-41 w/o 5.6.91	A21-104 w/o 18.11.87
A21-42 w/o 2.8.90	A21-106 w/o 19.5.92

Top right: All three Royal Australian Air Force F/A-18 squadrons often play host to foreign units. This Sea Harrier FA.2 from 801 Naval Air Squadron disembarked HMS Illustrious and relocated to the air base at RAAF Pearce, Western Australia, to perform air combat manoeuvring sorties with the Hornet units. (RAAF – LAC Peter Battye)

Right: No.75 Squadron participated in Exercise Pitch Black in July 2002. Here, A21-31 departs from RAAF Amberley, South Queensland, for another sortie against Royal Singaporean Air Force Northrop Grumman F-5E Tiger IIs and Lockheed Martin F-16 Fighting Falcons. (RAAF – LAC Andrew Eddie)

Above: A mixed formation of F/A-18s from 2 Operational Conversion Unit (OCU) wait their turn to refuel from a Boeing 707 tanker transport in September 2001. All aircrew training is performed by the unit, which has been based at RAAF Williamtown, New South Wales, since 1958, when the Sabre Trials Flight of 2 OTU was renumbered. (RAAF)

Bottom left No.3 Squadron has operated a mixture of types over the last 50 years, including the North American P-51 Mustang, which was licence-built by the Commonwealth Aircraft Corporation (CAC) as the CA-18 Mustang Mk.22. The unit also operated Gloster Meteor F.8s before converting to the Rolls-Royce Avon-engined CAC F-86 Sabre in March 1956. The squadron moved to Butterworth Malaya in late 1958 and flew operational missions during the Malayan campaign. F/A-18A, A21-47 was photographed at the biennial Airshow Down Under at Avalon in March 1995. (Key – Dave Allport)

75 Squadron

Right: During the Korean War, 77 Squadron operated both North American and CAC-built Mustangs before converting to Gloster Meteor F.8s, which the squadron subsequently used to shoot down four Mikoyan MiG-15s. The unit converted to the CAC-built version of the F-86 in November 1956 and joined 3 Squadron at Butterworth for the Malayan campaign. It remained permanently based there until early 1988. These two 77 Squadron F/A-18s are painted in an experimental darker grey colour scheme.
Top right: 1 (Nigel Pittaway)
Right: 2 (Jim Winchester)

77 Squadron

Right: The Aircraft Research and Development Unit performs flight trials for the various software and avionics systems upgrades the RAAF Hornet fleet will undergo as part of the HUG programme. Included in this upgrade are AIM-132 ASRAAM. (RAAF – ARDU)

Below: An F/A-18A from 77 Squadron flying over two famous Sydney landmarks, the Opera House and the Harbour Bridge. (RAAF via Nigel Pittaway)

409 Squadron, Canadian Forces

425 Squadron, Canadian Forces

410 Squadron, Canadian Forces

Above: All the aircraft that took part in the Operation Allied Force detachment to Aviano had their individual squadron markings removed – these were eventually replaced by a cartoon drawing of a rat to represent the unit detachment's name, the 'Balkan Rats'. (Boeing)

Below: The Aerospace Engineering Test Establishment (AETE) is based at Cold Lake, Alberta, alongside three regular fighter

squadrons. One of the aircraft it operates is this CF-18B, which is permanently assigned to undertake trials and other verification work. Due to the numerous modifications the aircraft has undergone, it is now so different to service aircraft that it will spend the rest of its working life as a test airframe. It was repainted in a smart red, white and blue colour scheme during 2001. (Canadian Forces)

433 Squadron, Canadian Forces

416 Squadron, Canadian Forces

439 Squadron, Canadian Forces

421 Squadron, Canadian Forces

441 Squadron, Canadian Forces

CANADA

Canadian Forces/Forces Canadiennes

410 Squadron	'Cougars'	CFB Cold Lake
416 Squadron	'Lynxes'	CFB Cold Lake
425 Squadron	'Alouettes'	CFB Bagotville
433 Squadron	'Porcupines'	CFB Bagotville
441 Squadron	'Silver Foxes'	CFB Cold Lake
AETE		CFB Cold Lake

Disbanded units

409 Squadron	'Nighthawks'	disbanded 1991
421 Squadron	'Red Indians'	disbanded 1992
439 Squadron	'Tigers'	disbanded 1992

F/A-18A (Canadian designation CF-188/CF-18A)
188701 to 188798

F/A-18B (Canadian designation CF-188/CF-18B)
188901 to 188940

Losses

188704 w/o 11.1.89	188765 w/o 17.4.90
188713 w/o 15.6.95	188768 w/o 14.8.96
188714 w/o 5.7.95	188772 w/o 22.4.90
188715 w/o 12.4.84	188773 w/o 5.4.88
188717 w/o 24.5.86	188779 w/o 17.4.90
188721 w/o 21.9.87	188792 w/o 4.4.90
188726 w/o 21.1.90	188919 w/o 4.5.87
188737 w/o 4.8.85	

Above right: A pair of Hornets fly over a snow-covered mountain during a routine training mission over Lapland in Northern Finland in March 2000. (Jyrki Laukkanen)

Right: The Finnish Air Force often practises dispersed operations from roads throughout the country. This aircraft from HävLLv 31 is seen operating from one such site in June 2002. (Jyrki Laukkanen)

Below right: This F/A-18D from HavLLv 21 shows its naval roots with its wings folded while awaiting its next mission on the flight-line at Tampere-Pirkkala in 1997. (Key – Alan Warnes)

FINLAND

Suomen Ilmaviotmat (Finnish Air Force)

Lapin Lennosto (LapLsto)/Lapland Air Command
Hävittäjälentolaivue (HavLLv) 11   Rovaniemi

Satakunnan Lennosto (SatLsto)/Satakunta Air Command
Hävittäjälentolaivue (HavLLv) 21   Tampere-Pirkkala

Karjalan Lennosto (KarLsto)/Karelian Air Command
Hävittäjälentolaivue (HavLLv) 31   Kuopio-Rissala
Ilmavoimien Koelentokeskus (KoeLntk)/Air Force
Flight Test Center   Halli

F-18C	**F-18D**
HN-401 to HN-457	HN-461 to HN-467

Losses
HN-430 w/o 8.11.01

Left: In August 2001, HavLLv 31 hosted Royal Air Force Harriers from 20 (Reserve) Squadron at RAF Wittering, Cambridgeshire, as part of Exercise Lone Kestrel. A VC.10 C.1K from 10 Squadron at RAF Brize Norton, Oxfordshire, provided tanker support for the six Harriers during the trip to Rovaniemi, a bonus for the Finnish Hornet crews who got their first opportunity to practice air-to-air refuelling.
(RAF – 20[R] Squadron)

Centre: Two F-18Cs from HavLLv 21 escort three Boeing F-15s from the 48th Fighter Wing based at RAF Lakenheath, Suffolk, into Tampere-Pirkkala shortly before an air show in June 1997.
(Jyrki Laukkanen)

Bottom: The three Finnish Air Force fighter squadrons are divided into three flights, two of them flying Hornets, while the third currently flies BAE SYSTEMS' Hawk Mk.51/51A trainers as combat aircraft.
(Jyrki Laukkanen)

11 Squadron

21 Squadron

31 Squadron

9 Squadron

25 Squadron

Above: This is the first-production Kuwait F/A-18C, seen during its ferry flight to Kuwait on January 25, 1992. All the aircraft were initially delivered to Kuwait international airport, where 25 Squadron commenced its work-up to operational status, followed by No.9 Squadron. Once the air bases that were badly damaged during Operation Desert Storm were repaired, both units relocated. (McDonnell Douglas)

Below: McDonnell Douglas borrowed this 25 Squadron F/A-18D to perform flying displays for potential customers at the Dubai air show in 1993. Kuwaiti Hornets have flown missions supporting Operation Southern Watch since 1993. (Key Archive)

KUWAIT	
Al Quwwat al Jawwiya al Kuwaitiya (Kuwait Air Force)	
9 Squadron	Ahmed al Jaber
25 Squadron	Ali al Salem
F/A-18C	**F/A-18D**
401 to 432	441 to 448

MALAYSIA		
Tentara Udara Diraja Malaysia (Royal Malaysian Air Force)		
1st Air Division		
18 Skuadron 'Lipan'	No.6 Air Base	Butterworth
F/A-18D		
M45-01 to M45-08		

Right: The Royal Malaysian Air Force purchased eight aircraft for maritime and night attack missions. It is the only F/A-18 operator to have painted all its aircraft in this dark grey colour scheme. Four aircraft were delivered on March 19, 1997, with the remaining four following in August. (McDonnell Douglas)

Right: The last production Malaysian aircraft on the 18 Squadron flightline at Butterworth during an Air Forces Monthly visit in April 1998. Malaysia intended to purchase an additional 12 aircraft but this was postponed due to the Asian financial crisis of the late 1990s. (Key – Alan Warnes)

Above: The Spanish Air Force uses the official designation 'C' for single-seat Hornets and 'CE' for two-seat aircraft they are also known by the designation EF-18, the 'E' referring to España for Spain, while the aircraft is the 15th fighter type operated by the Air Force. (Key - Steve Fletcher)

SPAIN
Ejértico del Aire Español (Spanish Air Force)
Ala 12 Torrejón
Escuadrón 121
Escuadrón 122
Escuadrón 124   disbanded 1994
Ala 15 Zaragoza
Escuadrón 151
Escuadrón 152
Escuadrón 153
Ala 11 Morón
Grupo 11
Escuadrón 111
Ala 46 Gando
Escuadrón 462
F/A-18A (Spanish designation EF-18A/A+)
C.15-13 to C.15-72
F/A-18B (Spanish designation EF-18B/B+)
CE.15-1 to CE.15-12

SURPLUS USN/USMC F/A-18AS TRANSFERRED TO SPAIN			
161936	C.15-73	162421	C.15-89
162415	C.15-74	162474	C.15-90
162416	C.15-75	161926	C.15-91
162426	C.15-76	161935	C.15-92
162446	C.15-77	161954	C.15-93
162471	C.15-78	161958	C.15-94
161940	C.15-79	161977	C.15-95
161944	C.15-80	162444	C.15-96
161949	C.15-81		
162456	C.15-82	**Losses**	
162461	C.15-83	C.15-17 w/o 16.8.94	
162465	C.15-84	C.15-19 w/o 7.11.88	
161951	C.15-85	C.15-42 w/o 15.3.00	
161939	C.15-86	C.15-63 w/o 15.3.00	
161950	C.15-87	C.15-71 w/o 28.11.91	
161953	C.15-88	C.15-91 w/o 11.2.03	

Centre: Two EF-18As from Ala 15 escorting a pair of Lockheed Martin F-16Cs from the Aviano-based 510th Fighter Squadron over Zaragoza in February 2002.(USAF – T/Sgt Dave Ahlschwede)

Left: This EF-18B was photographed landing at RAF Waddington in July 2001, during the three-week European air defence exercise NOMAD, which often includes both Spanish and Swiss Air Force Hornets. It still wears its US Navy Bureau Number (162902) on the fuselage, just above the Spanish Air Force roundel. (Key-Steve Fletcher)

Right: The first F-18D was handed over to the Swiss Air Force at Emmen on January 23, 1997. The second production aircraft is seen here performing a loop over the Lej de Segl shortly after entering service. (©Swiss Air Force)

Centre: The Swiss Air Force currently operates the Hornet in the air defence role and officially refers to the aircraft as the F-18. In wartime, the aircraft would be dispersed to various airfields across the country. Several of these airfields have large hangars carved out of the side of nearby mountains, where the aircraft stored inside can be suspended from the roof to save space. (©Swiss Air Force)

Below: This pair of F-18Cs pose for the camera while flying over the Alps in June 2001. The Swiss make regular deployments to RAF Waddington, Lincolnshire, to use the BAE SYSTEMS' North Sea Range (NSR). (©Swiss Air Force)

SWITZERLAND	
Schweizerische Flugwaffe (Swiss Air Force)	
Fliegerstaffel 11	Dübendorf
Fliegerstaffel 17	Payerne
Fliegerstaffel 18	Payerne
F-18C	**F-18D**
J-5001 to J-5026	J-5231 to J-5238
Losses	
J-5231 w/o 7.4.98	

Left: Until the F-18 entered service, the Swiss relied on both the Dassault Mirage IIIS and the Northrop Grumman F-5 Tiger II for the country's air defence, while the Hawker Hunter was tasked with the ground attack role. (©Swiss Air Force)

Centre left: Switzerland is currently planning to purchase up to 30 new fighter aircraft to replace the remaining F-5s by 2010. It is expected that the type will be chosen in either 2005 or 2006. In the meantime, the remaining Hornets are due to undergo a life extension and communications upgrade programme, enabling them to serve until around 2025. The Swiss also plan to purchase the AIM-9X Sidewinder. (©Swiss Air Force)

Bottom: Once the Hornets entered service and were declared fully operational, the Mirage IIIS was retired from service. Air Force pilots are split into two categories – the only pilots allowed to fly the Hornets are the professional pilots assigned to the Escadre de Surveillance (Surveillance Wing). The F-5s are flown by pilots from the reserve forces known as the Militiamen. These two Hornets are seen intercepting a German Air Force Transall C-160 in 1999. (©Swiss Air Force)

Above: One of the latest projects for which NASA has used its fleet of F/A-18s is the Automated Aerial Refuelling (AAR) trials, in which the aircraft carries the refuelling pod similar to the one used by Super Hornets. The aim of this study is to develop an aerodynamic model for the possibility of automated aerial refuelling of certain types such as Unmanned Aerial Vehicles (UAV). The aircraft is flying over the Dryden Flight Research Center, California, with the well-known Rogers dry lake bed in the background. (NASA – Carla Thomas)

Above right: Initial flight trials for the Automated Aerial Refuelling project progressed quickly, with two aircraft performing refuelling trials on December 19, 2002. (NASA – Lori Losey)

Right: The Active Aeroelastic Wing (AAW) trials programme commenced on November 15, 2002. Following this, a further series of check-out and parameter identification flights will be performed to obtain essential data for the development of new flight control software before a second series of tests begins. (NASA – Carla Thomas)

NATIONAL AERONAUTICS AND SPACE ADMINISTRATION			
Active aircraft			
161519	N843NA	161703	N850NA
160781	N845NA	161705	N851NA
161355	N846NA	161217	N852NA
161520	N847NA	161744	N853NA
Non airworthy or retired aircraft			
160780	N840NA preserved at the Virginia Air and Space Center, Hampton Virginia		
161216	N841NA returned to Navy		
161214	N842NA preserved Lancaster California		
161250	N843NA returned to Navy		
161251	This aircraft is used only as non-flying system tests airframe		
Losses			
161213	N844NA w/o 7.10.88		

Below; One of the standard F/A-18 chase planes performs for the camera in October 2002. Although the NASA aircraft are some of the oldest Hornets flying, there does not appear to be any replacement due and they look set to continue test-flying for many years. (NASA – Jim Ross)

Marine Fighter Attack
Squadron 251

Left: Although the F/A-18D has an excellent unrefuelled range, air-to-air refuelling is an essential capability for modern tactical aircraft. Here an aircraft of El Toro-based VMFA-225 refuels from a KC-130 over Arizona during the US Marine Corps Combat Readiness Evaluation-Scorpian Wind.

Left: VMFA-112 is currently based at the Joint Reserve Base at NAS Fort Worth, Texas, formerly known as NAS Dallas. The 'Cowboys' were the last Navy or Marines Corps' unit to fly the McDonnell Douglas F-4 Phantom II, finally converting to the F/A-18A in 1992. (Key – Alan Warnes)

Below: All the Marines Corps units based at El Toro, California, relocated to the former Navy base at Miramar, California, including VMFA-134. (Key – Alan Warnes)

Top: VMFA (AW)-225 formed as VMF-225 in January 1943, flying the Vought F4U Corsair until it converted to the Douglas Skyraider in 1954. In 1958, the unit began conversion to its first jet aircraft, the Douglas A-4D Skyhawk, becoming VMA-225 in the process. While operating the 'Scooter', it became the first unit to deploy and conduct night operations from USS *Enterprise*, from which it operated during the Cuban missile crisis of 1962. The unit flew the A-4 during the early years of the Vietnam War before converting to the all-weather-capable Grumman A-6E Intruder in 1966. As a result, the unit designation was changed again to became VMA (AW)-225. Following deactivation in 1972, the squadron had to wait until July 1991 before being reactivated to operate the F/A-18D. This aircraft was photographed while visiting the famous air races at Reno, Nevada, in September 2000. (Key – Duncan Cubitt)

Above right: The 'Red Devils' of VMFA-232 is the oldest and most decorated active fighter attack unit in the Marines, formally commissioning on September 1, 1925, flying the Vought VE-7. During the squadron's lifetime, it has flown an interesting array of aircraft, including the Douglas SBD Dauntless, Grumman TBF Avenger and Vought F4U Corsair. In March 1953, the unit entered the jet age with the Grumman F9F Panther, flying this from El Toro until it relocated to Kaneohe Bay, Hawaii, in 1954, initially flying the North American FJ-2 Fury. After converting to the FJ-4 in 1956, it became the first unit in the Marine Corps to qualify with the AIM-9 Sidewinder and in air-to-air refuelling. Other well-known types flown by VMFA-232 include the Vought F-8 Crusader from 1958 to 1967, when it transitioned to the McDonnell Douglas F-4 Phantom II which it flew until December 1988, when it prepared to convert to the F/A-18A. (Key – Alan Warnes)

UNITED STATES MARINE CORPS

Marine Air Group (MAG)-11 — Marine Corps Air Station Miramar, California

VMFA (AW)-121	'Green Knights'	F/A-18D	VK
VMFA (AW)-225	'Vikings'	F/A-18D	CE
VMFA-232	'Red Devils'	F/A-18C	WT
VMFA (AW)-242	'Bats'	F/A-18D	DT
VMFA-314	'Black Knights'	F/A-18C	VW
VMFA-323	'Death Rattlers'	F/A-18C	WS
VMFAT-101	'Sharpshooters'	F/A-18A/B/C/D	SH

Marine Air Group (MAG)-31 — Marine Corps Air Station Beaufort, South Carolina

VMFA-115	'Silver Eagles'	F/A-18A+	VE
VMFA-122	'Crusaders'	F/A-18C	DC
VMFA (AW)-224	'Bengals'	F/A-18D	WK
VMFA-251	'Thunderbolts'	F/A-18C	DW
VMFA-312	'Checkerboards'	F/A-18A+	DR
VMFA (AW)-332	'Moonlighters'	F/A-18D	EA
VMFA (AW)-533	'Hawks'	F/A-18D	ED

Marine Air Group (MAG)-12 — MCAS Iwakuni, Japan

VMFA-212	'Lancers'	F/A-18C	WD

USMC Reserve units
Marine Air Group (MAG-41) — NAS Fort Worth, Texas

VMFA-112	'Cowboys'	F/A-18A	MA

Marine Air Group (MAG-42) — NAS Atlanta, Georgia

VMFA-142	'Flying Gators'	F/A-18A	MB

Marine Air Group (MAG-46) — MCAS Miramar, California

VMFA-134	'Smoke'	F/A-18A	MF

Marine Air Group (MAG-49) — NAF Washington/Andrews AFB

VMFA-321	'Hell's Angels'	F/A-18A	MG

Former US Marine Corps F/A-18 Units

VMFA-235	'Death Angels'	DB	Disestablished	June 30, 1996
VMFA-333	'Shamrocks'	DN	Disestablished	March 31, 1992
VMFA-451	'Warlords'	VM	Disestablished	January 31, 1997
VMFA-531	'Grey Ghosts'	EC	Disestablished	March 31, 1992

Marine Fighter Attack Squadron 314

Marine Fighter Attack Squadron 321

Marine Fighter Attack Squadron 531 (Disbanded)

Top: This colourful F/A-18C was assigned to VMFA-251, operating from USS *Theodore Roosevelt* during Operation Enduring Freedom in November 2001. (Key – Alan Warnes)

Above left: When VMFA-314 operates from its home base at MCAS Miramar its aircraft wear the VW code on the tail. This aircraft was photographed at Miramar in October 1996. (Key – Alan Warnes)

Above left: The Commanding Officer of VMFA-314, the 'Black Knights', makes his 700th arrested landing in an F/A-18 aboard USS *John C Stennis* on April 10, 2002, while conducting combat missions in support of Operation Enduring Freedom. (USN – Ph3 Joshua Word)

Left: This VMFA-323 F/A-18C is armed with an AGM-65 Maverick air-to-surface missile. (Tony Holmes)

Above: VMFAT-101 are often deployed aboard carriers to give pilots carrier qualification training. This F/A-18D is about to be launched from one of the catapults on USS *John C Stennis* in July 2001. (USN – PH3 William K Fletcher)

Above: All three units from Carrier Air Wing 2 are visible in this photo, taken during a cruise aboard USS *Constellation* in May 2001. Visible from the top are VMFA-323 'Death Rattlers', with VFA-137 'Kestrels' in the middle and VFA-151 'Vigilantes' at the bottom. (Tony Holmes)

Right: The 'Fighting Redcocks' of VFA-22 were originally established as VF-63 during July 1948, performing three tours during the Korean War, between 1950 and 1952. The unit was re-designated VA-63 for a short period in March 1956, before it became VA-22 in July 1959. During the first ten years, it flew various types including the Grumman F8F-2 Bearcat, Vought F4U-4 Corsair, entering the jet age with the Grumman F9F Panther and later the Grumman F9F Cougar. The squadron also flew several versions of the Douglas A-4 Skyhawk and the Ling Temco Vought (LTV) A-7E Corsair II until it converted to the F/A-18C in 1990. VFA-22 was formerly assigned to Carrier Air Wing 11 until replaced by VFA-14 and VFA-41 in 2002. It was initially due to join Carrier Air Wing 8, but joined CVW-9 in early 2003. The squadron commander's aircraft is seen flying over the Fort Jefferson National Monument, which served as a prison until 1874 and is located within the Dry Tortugas National Park 60 miles (97km) west of Key West in the Gulf of Mexico, on June 3, 2002. (USN – Lt Cmdr Creighton Holt)

Right: A pilot from VFA-146 expends flares from his F/A-18C over the Pacific Ocean during a training exercise on August 16, 1999. (USN – Lt Karl Rauch)

UNITED STATES NAVY

US Sixth Fleet (Atlantic)

Oceana Naval Air Station, Virginia

VFA-15	'Valions'	F/A-18C	VFA-87	'Golden Warriors'	F/A-18C
VFA-34	'Blue Blasters'	F/A-18C	VFA-105	'Gunslingers'	F/A-18C
VFA-37	'Bulls'	F/A-18C	VFA-106	'Gladiators'	FA-18A/B/C/D
VFA-81	'Sunliners'	F/A-18C	VFA-131	'Wildcats'	F/A-18C
VFA-83	'Rampagers'	F/A-18C	VFA-136	'Knighthawks'	F/A-18C

Marine Corps Air Station Beaufort, South Carolina

VFA-82	'Marauders'	F/A-18C
VFA-86	'Sidewinders'	F/A-18C

US Seventh Fleet (Pacific)

Lemoore Naval Air Station, California

VFA-14	'Top Hatters'	F/A-18E
VFA-22	'Fighting Redcocks'	F/A-18C
VFA-25	'Fist of the Fleet'	F/A-18C
VFA-41	'Black Aces'	F/A-18F
VFA-94	'Mighty Shrikes'	F/A-18C
VFA-97	'Warhawks'	F/A-18A
VFA-102	'Diamondbacks'	F/A-18F
VFA-113	'Stingers'	F/A-18C
VFA-115	'Eagles'	F/A-18E
VFA-122	'Flying Eagles'	F/A-18E/F (FRS)
VFA-125	'Rough Raiders'	F/A-18A/B/C/D (FRS)
VFA-137	'Kestrels'	F/A-18C
VFA-146	'Blue Diamonds'	F/A-18C
VFA-147	'Argonauts'	F/A-18C
VFA-151	'Vigilantes'	F/A-18C

Atsugi Naval Air Facility, Japan

VFA-27	'Chargers'	F/A-18C
VFA-192	'Golden Dragons'	F/A-18C
VFA-195	'Dambusters'	F/A-18C

Naval Air Systems Command

Naval Air Strike Warfare Center	'Strike'	F/A-18A/B	NAS Fallon, Nevada

Naval Air Warfare Center – Aircraft Division Atlantic

NAS Patuxent River, Maryland

VX-23		Operates all six versions of the F/A-18 Family
USN Test Pilot School		F/A-18B

Naval Air Warfare Center – Aircraft Division Pacific

Naval Weapons Test Squadron-China Lake

VX-9	'Vampires'	F/A-18A/B/C/D/E/F
VX-31	'Dust Devils'	F/A-18A/B/D/E/F

Naval Air Force Reserve

NAF Atlanta, Georgia

VFA-201	'Hunters'	F/A-18ANAS	Fort Worth JRB
VFA-203	'Blue Dolphins'	F/A-18A+	NAS Atlanta
VFA-204	'River Rattlers'	F/A-18A	NAS New Orleans JRB
VFC-12	'Fighting Omars'	F/A-18A	NAS Oceana

Command Naval Air Training Command (CNATRA) NAS Corpus Christi, Texas

Naval Flight Demonstration Squadron	'The Blue Angels'	F/A-18A/B	NAS Pensacola, Florida

Left: Carrier Air Wing 11 spent the latter part of 2002 working up for its cruise to the Western Pacific (WestPac) aboard USS *Nimitz*. The Air Wing for this cruise included all three generations of the F/A-18 family assigned to four squadrons. Of these, both VFA-14 and VFA-41 performed their first Super Hornet deployment using the 'E and 'F model. VFA-94 continued to fly the F/A-18C, while VFA-97 made one of its last active the last active deployments flying the F/A-18A. (USN – Airman Mark Rebilas)

Right: The F/A-18 community reached the five millionth flight hour in early December 2002. VFA-192 was among the first F/A-18 units to commemorate the event when it flew past Mount Fuji in Japan with this neat three-ship formation on December 12. The unit credited with flying the 5,000,000th flight hour was VMFA-312, based at MCAS Beaufort flying the F/A-18A+. (USN – Lt Cmdr William Koyama)

Strike Fighter Squadron 102

Strike Fighter Squadron 106

Strike Fighter Squadron 131

Naval Flight Demonstration Squadron 'The Blue Angels'

Above: An F/A-18C assigned to the 'Wildcats' of VFA-131 strains on the catapult prior to launching from USS *John F Kennedy*, while supporting Operation Enduring Freedom on April 27, 2002. (USN – PMA Joshua Karsten)

US NAVY & MARINE CORPS F/A-18 SQUADRON CARRIER AIR WINGS (CVW) ASSIGNMENTS 2003/2004	
US Atlantic Fleet	
CVW-1 AB	**CVW-8 AJ**
VFA-82	VFA-15
VFA-86	VFA-87
VMFA-312	VFA-201
	CVW-17 AA
CVW-3 AC	VFA-34
VFA-37	VFA-81
VFA-105	VFA-83
VMFA-115	
	Fleet Replenishment Squadron (FRS) AD
CVW-7 AG	
VFA-131	VFA-106
VFA-136	

US NAVY & MARINE CORPS F/A-18 SQUADRON CARRIER AIR WINGS (CVW) ASSIGNMENTS 2003/2004	
US Pacific Fleet	
CVW-2 NE	VFA-94
VFA-137	VFA-97
VFA-151	
VMFA-323	**CVW-14 NK**
	VFA-25
CVW-5 NF	VFA-113
VFA-27	VFA-115
VFA-192	
VFA-195	**Fleet Replenishment Squadrons (FRS) NJ**
CVW-9 NG	VFA-22
VFA-22	VFA-125
VFA-146	
VFA-147	**US Naval Reserve AF**
VMFA-314	CVWR-20
	VFA-201
CVW-11 NH	VFA-203
VFA-14	VFA-204
VFA-41	VMFA-142

US NAVY AIRCRAFT CARRIERS

CV-41	USS *Midway* [1]
CV-43	USS *Coral Sea* [1]
CV-59	USS *Forrestal* [1]
CV-60	USS *Saratoga* [1]
CV-61	USS *Ranger* [1][2]
CV-62	USS *Independence* [1]
CV-63	USS *Kitty Hawk*
CV-64	USS *Constellation* [1]
CVN-65	USS *Enterprise*
CV-66	USS *America* [1]
CV-67	USS *John F Kennedy*
CVN-68	USS *Nimitz*
CVN-69	USS *Dwight D Eisenhower*
CVN-70	USS *Carl Vinson*
CVN-71	USS *Theodore Roosevelt*
CVN-72	USS *Abraham Lincoln*
CVN-73	USS *George Washington*
CVN-74	USS *John C Stennis*
CVN-75	USS *Harry S Truman*
CVN-76	USS *Ronald Reagan*
CVN-77	USS *George H W Bush*

[1] Decommissioned

[2] F/A-18s have never operated from this carrier

FORMER US NAVY F/A-18 UNITS

VF-45	'Blackbirds'	March 31, 1996
VFA-127	'Desert Bogeys'	March 31, 1996
VFA-132	'Privateers'	June 1, 1992
VFA-161	'Chargers'	April 1, 1988
VFA-303	'Goldenhawks'	December 31, 1994
VFA-305	'Lobos'	December 31, 1994
VAQ-34	'Electric Horsemen'	October 1, 1993
VX-4XF	'Evaluators'	September 30, 1994
VX-5XE	'Vampires'	April 29, 1994
Pacific Missile Test Center		May 8, 1995
Naval Weapons Center		May 8, 1995

DISESTABLISHED CARRIER AIR WINGS

CVW-10	NM	June 1, 1988
CVW-13	AK	January 1, 1991
CVW-6	AE	April 1,1992
CVWR-30	ND	December 31, 1994
CVW-15	NL	December 31, 1995

Strike Fighter Squadron 136 (Desert version)

Strike Fighter Squadron 136

Strike Fighter Squadron 147

Strike Fighter Squadron 146

Below: The squadron commanders F/A-18C from the 'Blue Diamonds' of VFA-146 wore this patriotic colour scheme while the unit operated from USS *John C Stennis* in April 2002. (USN – Lt Kyle Turco)

SHAred Reconnaissance Pod logo

Left: One of the F/A-18s assigned to Carrier Air Wing 17 aboard USS *George Washington* launches from the flight deck during early evening flight operations. (USN – PH2 Corey T Lewis)

US HORNET SERIALS

Northrop YF-17
72-1569
72-1570

YF-18A
160775 to 160780
160782 to 160783
160785

TF-18A/YF/A-18B
160781
160784

F/A-18A
161213 – 161216
161248
161250 – 161251
161353
161358 – 161359
161361 – 161367
161519 – 161528
161702 – 161703
161705 – 161706
161708 – 161710
161712 – 161713
161715 – 161718
161720 – 161722
161724 – 161726
161728 – 161732
161734 – 161739
161741 – 161745
161747 – 161761
161925 – 161931
161933 – 161937
161939 – 161942
161944 – 161946
161948 – 161987
162394 – 162401
162403 – 162407
162409 – 162412
162414 – 162418
162420 – 162426
162428 – 162477
162826 – 162835
162837 – 162841
162843 – 162845
162847 – 162849
162851 – 162856
162858 – 162863
162865 – 162869
162871 – 162875
162877 – 162884
162886 – 162909
163092 – 163103
163105 – 163109
163111 – 163114
163116 – 163122
163124 – 163175

F/A-18B
161217
161249
161354 – 161357
161360
161704
161707
161711
161714
161719
161723
161727
161733
161740
161746
161924

161932
161938
161943
161947
162402
162408
162413
162419
162427
162836
163842
163846
163850
163857
163864
163870
163876
163885
163104
163110
163115
163123

F/A-18C
163427 – 163433
163435
163437 – 163440
163442 – 163444
163446
163448 – 163451
163453
163455 – 163456
163458 – 163459
163461 – 163463
163465 – 163467
163469 – 163471
163473
163475 – 163478
163480 – 163481
163483 – 163485
163487
163489 – 163491
163493 – 163496
163498 – 163499
163502 – 163506
163508 – 163509
163699
163701 – 163706
163708 – 163719
163721 – 163733
163735 – 163748
163750 – 163762
163764 – 163770
163772 – 163777
163779 – 163782
163985
163987 – 163988
163990
163992 – 163993
163995 – 163996
163998 – 163999
164000
164002 – 164004
164006 – 164008
164010
164012 – 164013
164015 – 164016
164018
164020 – 164021
164023
164025
164027
164029 – 164031
164033 – 164034
164036 – 164037
164039

164041 – 164042
164044 – 164045
164047 – 164048
164050
164052
164054 – 164055
164057
164059 – 164060
164062 – 164063
164065 – 164067
164197
164199 – 164202
164204 – 164206
164208 – 164210
164212 – 164215
164217 – 164218
164220 – 164223
164225 – 164227
164229 – 164232
164234 – 164236
164238 – 164240
164242 – 164244
164246 – 164248
164250 – 164253
164255 – 164258
164260 – 164262
164264 – 164266
164268 – 164271
164273 – 164278
164627 – 164648
164654 – 164655
164657 – 164658
164660 – 164661
164663 – 164664
164666
164668 – 164669
164671
164673
164675 – 164676
164678
164680 – 164682
164684
164686 – 164687
164689
164691
164693
164695 – 164698
164700 – 164701
164703 – 164704
164706 – 164710
164712 – 164713
164715 – 164716
164718 – 164722
164724 – 164725
164727 – 164728
164730 – 164734
164736 – 164737
164739 – 164740
164865
164867
164869
164871
164873
164877
164879
164881
164883
164885
164887
164889 – 164897
164899 – 164900
164902 – 164912
164946
164948
164950
164952

164954
164956
164958
164960
164962
164964
164966
164968 – 164980
165171 – 165230
165399 – 165404
165406 – 165408
165526

F/A-18D
163434
163436
163441
163445
163447
163452
163454
163457
163460
163464
163468
163472
163474
163479
163482
163486
163488
163492
163497
163500 – 163501
163507
163510
163700
163707
163720
163734
163749
163763
163771
163778
163986
163989
163991
163994
163997
164001
164005
164009
164011
164014
164017
164019
164022
164024
164026
164028
164032
164035
164038
164040
164043
164046
164049
164051
164053
164056
164058
164061
164064
164068
164196
164198

164203
164207
164211
164216
164219
164224
164233
164237
164241
164245
164249
164254
164259
164263
164267
164272
164279
164649 – 164653
164656
164659
164662
164665
164667
164670
164672
164674
164677
164679
164683
164685
164688
164690
164692
164694
164699
164702
164705
164711
164714
164717
164723
164726
164729
164735
164738
164866
164868
164870
164872
164874
164876
164878
164880
164882
164884
164886
164888
164898
164901
164945
164947
164949
164951
164953
164955
164957
164959
164961
164963
164965
164967
165405
165409 – 165416
165527 – 165532
165681

SUPER HORNET SERIALS	
F/A-18E	**F/A-18F**
Prototypes	Prototypes
165164 – 165165	165166
165167 – 165169	165170
Production	Production
165533 – 165540	165541 – 165544
165660 – 165667	165668 – 165679
165779 – 165792	165793 – 165808
165860 – 165874*	165875 – 165894*

*These aircraft fall within the mixed block allocation
165860 – 165937
166420 – 166467 are allocated to both models

Top: In August 2002 several units from Carrier Air Wing 5 deployed to Andersen Air Force Base (AFB) on the island of Guam, to conduct training on a weapons range at Farallon de Medinilla, an uninhabited island 150 miles (240km) to the north of Guam. This F/A-18C from VFA-27 the 'Royal Maces' launches during the first phase of the exercise, when it operated alongside VFA-192, dropping both live and practice ordnance.
(USAF – Airman Joshua Strang)

Left: The 'Blue Dolphins' of VFA-203 are assigned to Reserve Carrier Air Wing 20, flying the upgraded F/A-18A+. One of the unit's aircraft is about to be launched from USS *Harry S Truman* during one of the Annual Fleet Week air and sea power displays held by the US Navy. (USN – PMA Audrey L Roberts)

Left: When the 'Black Aces' of VFA-41 commenced its first deployment with a new aircraft in 2003, it also marked the introduction of the new SHAred Reconnaissance Pod (SHARED).
(USN – PH3 Yesenia Rosas)

Left: The three F/A-18C squadrons from CVW-17 perform for the camera during a training mission. (USN – Capt Dana Potts)

Above: VFA-41 became the official Super Hornet demonstration squadron in 2002, taking over from VFA-122. One of the units F/A-18Fs appeared at the Farnborough air show in July. (Key – Duncan Cubitt)

Right: Aircraft from Carrier Air Wing 14 rest on USS *Abraham Lincoln*'s flight deck during a thunderstorm in the Arabian Sea at the beginning of November 2002. (USN – PH2 Aaron Ansarov)

Right: The US Navy Tailhook legacy flight performs at air shows throughout the USA every year, depending on the availability of pilots rated to fly piston-engined aircraft. The F/A-18D from VFA-125 keeps close formation with a Vought FG-1D Corsair, licence-built by Goodyear, and a Grumman F8F Bearcat. (Key – Duncan Cubitt)

LOSSES				
F-18A	162447 w/o 8.1.86	**F/A-18B**	163774 w/o 9.10.91	165209 w/o 16.9.98
160777 w/o 16.3.81	162450 w/o 8.12.87	161719 w/o 1.10.92	163995 w/o 17.1.96	165219 w/o 29.5.01
	162451 w/o 23.10.01	161727 w/o 20.5.87	164004 w/o 24.8.91	165223 w/o 25.9.98
TF-18A	162476 w/o 16.11.87	161932 w/o 28.10.99	164015 w/o 27.3.92	165399 w/o 4.12.99
160784 w/o 8.9.80	162477 w/o 9.10.87	162413 w/o 8.9.87	164031 w/o 7.5.92	16.... w/o 3.11.02
	162827 w/o 18.11.94		164044 w/o 28.1.95	
F/A-18A	162833 w/o 22.11.92	**F/A-18C**	164063 w/o 17.1.96	**F/A-18D**
161213 w/o 7.10.88	162845 w/o 15.3.92	163427 w/o 3.10.89	164065 w/o 4.12.91	163445 w/o 30.8.95
161215 w/o 14.11.86	162847 w/o 14.4.87	163428 w/o 15.2.90	164199 w/o 9.8.96	163454 w/o 4.3.92
161248 w/o 2.5.83	162852 w/o 6.10.91	163453 w/o 12.1.91	164213 w/o 12.8.93	163492 w/o 17.5.95
161363 w/o 16.3.85	162855 w/o 14.4.87	163466 w/o 17.7 96	164232 w/o 27.10.00	163707 w/o 14.8.90
161364 w/o 11.2.91	162858 w/o 31.3.90	163467 w/o 21.6.94	164248 w/o 12.8.91	163720 w/o 24.8.95
161522 w/o 12.2.87	162868 w/o 16.01.02	163475 w/o 6.10.90	164251 w/o 23.10.01	163749 w/o 14.11.02
161524 w/o 23.1.90	162887 w/o 15.3.02	163484 w/o 17.1.91	164260 w/o 24.7.92	163778 w/o 16.6.99
161734 w/o 24.4.95	162891 w/o 6.6.02	163489 w/o 8.2.98	164666 w/o 14.9.97	164035 w/o 29.5.92
161741 w/o 17.11.83	162908 w/o 22.6.89	163704 w/o 8.5.89	164681 w/o 29.9.00	164196 w/o 15.5.92
161927 w/o 15.1.96	163096 w/o 5.2.91	163710 w/o 20.8.91	164684 w/o 9.9.92	164207 w/o 9.2.97
161933 w/o 22.10.86	163109 w/o 28.1.88	163712 w/o 13.5.92	164695 w/o 18.11.94	164233 w/o 9.5.00
161966 w/o 19.6.84	163121 w/o 24.1.91	163713 w/o 16.10.90	164697 w/o 3.4.96	164665 w/o 10.1.00
161971 w/o 7.2.87	163125 w/o 28.5.92	163727 w/o 10.3.99	164706 w/o 21.5.93	164692 w/o 11.9.00
161974 w/o 22.8.96	163128 w/o 3.12.99	163729 w/o 8.3.91	164728 w/o 2.4.96	164868 w/o 7.7.00
161980 w/o 12.6.89	163134 w/o 22.8.01	163732 w/o 23.2.92	164737 w/o 20.10.00	164963 w/o 7.3.96
161987 w/o 4.6.87	163139 w/o 26.7.02	163739 w/o 9.5.89	164890 w/o 6.2.98	165682 w/o 17.1.03
162399 w/o 8.5.89	163136 w/o 28.1.88	163743 w/o 20.8.98	164894 w/o 6.2.98	
162404 w/o 17.7.85	163170 w/o 10.11.88	163744 w/o 27.4.98	164867 w/o 5.10.00	**F/A-18F**
162405 w/o 24.4.88	16.... w/o 17.12.02	163748 w/o 18.2.03	165178 w/o 27.5.98	165881 w/o 18.10.02
162441 w/o 22.6.93		163759 w/o 20.1.99	165180 w/o 4.12.96	165889 w/o 18.10.02
			165189 w/o 19.6.96	

F/A-18s have operated in various trouble spots throughout the world, predominately in the Middle East theatre of operations. The first time US Navy and Marine Corps Hornets participated in combat operations was during Operation Prairie Fire, off the Libyan coast in March 1986. America had already had several skirmishes with Libya after its leader Colonel Muammar Al-Qadhafi's decision to impose a 'line of death' around the entrance to the Gulf of Sirte.

The USA also claimed to have evidence that Libya was actively sponsoring terrorist activities and was involved with a bomb blast at a Berlin discotheque that had killed several US servicemen. As a result, on March 24 aircraft from Carrier Air Wing 13 embarked aboard USS *Coral Sea* commenced Combat Air Patrols (CAP) to protect the carrier battle group. During these operations within the Gulf area, which America had actually stated was inside international waters, F/A-18As from VFA-131, VFA-132, VMFA-314 and VMFA-323 regularly encountered a mix of Libyan AF fighters, including Dassault Mirage F1s,

Mikoyan MiG-23s and MiG-25s, and Sukhoi Su-22s. Meanwhile, radar installations at an SA-5 SAM site on the coast at Sirte had been illuminating US aircraft and the task of taking these out was given to the F/A-18s, this also marked the combat debut for both the Hornet and the Hughes AGM-88 HARM.

Within hours of Operation Prairie Fire concluding on April 14, a new mission – Operation Eldorado Canyon – began. Shortly before midnight, 16 Hornets were launched from the *Coral Sea*, eight of them armed with AGM-88As to perform SEAD duties, while the remainder performed Combat Air Patrols (CAP) off the coast. The main strike force, which consisted of Grumman A-6E Intruders and Ling-Temco-Vought (LTV) A-7E Corsair IIs from the *Coral Sea* and two other carriers, headed inland to destroy further targets around Benghazi.

While approaching their targets, they met heavy resistance from a mixture of different SAMs, including SA-2 Guideline, SA-3 Goa, SA-6 Gainful and SA-8 Gecko. The Hornets responded by firing a total of 16 HARMs, which led to the successful conclusion of the mission without loss. After Iraqi forces invaded Kuwait on August 2, 1990, the US Navy dispatched USS *Independence* with CVW-14 embarked, including VFA-25 and VFA-113, into the Gulf of Oman on August 8. At the same time USS *Dwight D Eisenhower* sailed through the Suez Canal, taking up station in the Red Sea, with VFA-131 and VFA-136 operating F/A-18As, embarked as part of CVW-7.

Below: Canadian Forces' CF-18s often intercepted long-range Soviet bombers transiting towards Cuba as part of their shared responsibilities within the North American Aerospace Defense mand (NORAD). This agreement between the two countries dates back to 1958 and is intended to inform either nation of imminent attack. Here, an aircraft from 425 Squadron at Bagotville, Quebec, follows a Tupolev Tu-142 Bear-F Mod 3 off the east coast of Canada.(Canadian Forces Photo)

Below: The Libyan Air Force put up a large and varied contingent of aircraft to intercept the US Navy during Operation Prairie Fire, including the feared Mikoyan MiG-25 Foxbats, one of which is seen in formation with a 'Black Knights' F/A-18 of VMFA-314. (USN – Robert F Dorr Collection)

Bottom: When the Air Wing aboard USS *Coral Sea* participated in NATO exercises in March 1986, this F/A-18A from VFA-132 intercepted an Italian Air Force Piaggio PD808 during Exercise Sardinia 86.(USN – Robert F Dorr Collection)

A day earlier, USS *Saratoga* had put to sea with CVW-17 embarked. Among the units on board were VFA-81 and VFA-83, both operating F/A-18Cs. With no signs of an Iraqi withdrawal from Kuwait, America dispatched more aircraft to what had now become Operation Desert Shield. These included several US Marine Corps F/A-18 squadrons. First to be deployed were F/A-18Cs from VMFA-235 at MCAS Kaneohe Bay, Hawaii, and F/A-18As from VMFA-314 from MCAS El Toro, California, on August 20, while F/A-18As from VMFA-333 and VMFA-451 at MCAS Beaufort followed on August 21.

As the weeks became months, several carriers were relieved of duty. First to return home was the *Eisenhower* in September, followed by the *Independence* in December. They were replaced by USS *Midway* in October, with units VFA-151, VFA-192 and VFA-195 all operating F/A-18As. Two more carriers sailed in December, including USS *America* with the F/A-18Cs of VFA-82 and VFA-86 from CVW-1 embarked, and USS *Theodore Roosevelt* with F/A-18As from VFA-15 and VFA-87, part of CVW-8. Canada also contributed to the multi-national forces by deploying 18 CF-18s to Doha in Qatar. The first of these aircraft were deployed on October 6, flown by crews from 409 Squadron, replaced in December by crews from 439 Squadron.

Eight more Canadian aircraft were deployed shortly before the start of Desert Storm. Three more Marine Corps units joined the other units deployed at Sheikh Isa Air base, Bahrain, including F/A-18Cs from VMFA-212 and VMFA-232, together with the recently-delivered F/A-18Ds of VMFA (AW)-121, bringing the total of USMC F/A-18s in the region to 84. Operation Desert Storm began on January 17, 1991. Navy F/A-18s flew various missions including Suppression of Enemy Air Defences (SEAD) and Combat Air Patrols (CAP). Although two aircraft were lost during the first two weeks, VFA-81 claimed two aerial victories when they shot down a pair of Mikoyan MiG-21s on the first night of operations, en route to attack an airfield. Lieutenant Commander Mark Fox, flying 163508, shot down one aircraft with an AIM-9 Sidewinder and Lieutenant Nick Mongillo, flying 163502, shot the second MiG down with an AIM-9. The Marines Hornets undertook Close Air Support (CAS) missions, supporting Marines on the ground, while F/A-18Ds performed in the Forward Air Control or Fast FAC role. Eight Marine Corps' aircraft were damaged by SAMs but all returned to base

Top: Both the Grumman A-6E Intruder and the F/A-18 were involved in action over Libya on the night of April 14, 1986, as part of Operation Eldorado Canyon. (USN – Robert F Dorr Collection)

Above middle: An F/A-18C from VFA-81 refuels from this USAF Boeing KC-135 Stratotanker, while four more aircraft from the squadron await their turn, along with a Grumman A-6E Intruder from VA-35 'Black Panthers'. (McDonnell Douglas)

Above: This F/A-18C from VFA-81, seen shortly before landing aboard USS *Saratoga*, is the aircraft that Lieutenant Nick Mongillo used to shoot down an Iraqi MiG-21 on January 17, 1991.(McDonnell Douglas)

Right: VMFA (AW)-121 was the only unit to fly the F/A-18D during Operation Desert Storm. One of its aircraft is seen flying over one of the many oil well head fires left by retreating Iraqi troops during the closing stages of the conflict. (McDonnell Douglas)

Left: One of the first units to use the FLIR-LTD/R in action was the 'Hawks' of VMFA (AW)-533, home-based at MCAS Beaufort, South Carolina, but forward-deployed to Aviano in Italy during operations over Bosnia. (McDonnell Douglas)

Left: All the F/A-18D units at Beaufort flew missions over Bosnia, including VMFA (AW)-224. One of its aircraft is seen in the Hardened Aircraft Shelters (HAS) at Aviano in May 1997, wearing the short-lived BM (Beaufort Marine) tail codes applied to Hornets based at Beaufort.
(Key – Duncan Cubitt)

Left: US Navy and US Marine Hornets squadrons have been heavily involved over both of the United Nations-designated No-Fly Zones imposed over the 36° Parallel over Northern Iraq and the 32° Parallel over Southern Iraq.
(USN – Christopher Mobley)

Left: A Marine Corps' pilot from VMFA-251 climbs into the cockpit of his F/A-18C aboard USS George Washington, cruising in the Persian Gulf in February 1998.
(USN – Brian Fleske)

safely. The Canadian Hornets flew both air-to-air and air-to-ground sorties, also protecting the Canadian task force and other naval vessels in the Persian Gulf. The detachment gained the nickname 'Desert Cats' while it was based at Doha. F/A-18s have also seen action over European skies, flying CAPs over Bosnia-Herzegovina during Operation Deny Flight. The intended aim of this was to prevent the Serbian Air Force assisting the army in its policy of ethnic cleansing during the worsening situation in the Former Republic of Yugoslavia.

The No-Fly Zones over Northern and Southern Iraq have been policed by F/A-18s and other aircraft since they were imposed during August 1992, and when several aircraft were challenged by Iraqi air defences on several occasions in December 1992. As a result of these incursions, a limited series of air strikes were launched over Southern Iraq on January 13, 1993. Hornets from USS *Kitty Hawk's* Air Wing were among the aircraft that attacked various radar installations and SAM sites, while Combat Air Patrols were flown by Kuwaiti Air Force Hornets. With no end in sight to the trouble in Bosnia, NATO launched Operation Blue Sword on April 10, 1994. The following day, two F/A-18As from VMFA-251 attacked a Serbian T55 tank that had been firing on Gorazde, using Mk.82 General purpose (GP) bombs. After destroying the tank, they strafed the area with 20mm gun fire, destroying a truck and three Armoured Personnel Carriers (APC).

Operation Disciplined Guard, in conjunction with the Deny Flight mission, followed in July to protect UN forces on the ground in Bosnia. The F/A-18s tasked with flying Operation Deny Flight missions were joined by eight VMFA (AW)-533 F/A-18Ds. These arrived at Aviano in July 1994, and worked with Navy Hornets aboard USS *Theodore Roosevelt* and other NATO aircraft. The start of the operation was greatly enhanced by the introduction of the Loral AN/AAS-38 NITE Hawk FLIR LTD/R pod. This development finally gave the USN and USMC F/A-18 community the ability to simultaneously illuminate and deliver laser-guided weapons. Both services had previously relied on the Grumman A-6E Intruder for this task.

The Serbs continued their attacks on the Bosnian people and, following attacks by Serbian AF SOKO IAR-93 Oraos on installations within UN designated safe areas, NATO launched an attack on Udbina airfield in the Serbian enclave of Krajina, inside Croatia, on November 21, 1994. Among the attacking aircraft were USMC F/A-18Ds from VMFA (AW)-332, who attacked a SAM site with AGM-88 HARMs. Spanish Air Force EF-18s joined the other NATO aircraft, arriving at Aviano in December 1994. It was not long before they began flying missions over Bosnia and were soon involved in combat operations when they joined Marine Corps' F/A-18Ds to attack weapons storage bunkers at a Serbian ammunition depot near Pale on May 25, 1995.

Below: The pilot of this F/A-18C from VMFA-312 awaits the launch signal from the flight deck officer prior to taking part in the second wave of air strikes during Operation Desert Fox in December 1998. (USN – Brian C McLaughlin)

Bottom left: This Spanish EF-18 from Ala 12 was based at Aviano during air operations over Kosovo and parts of the former Yugoslavia. (Key – Steve Fletcher)

Bottom right: Canadian Hornets participated in the air campaign over the former Yugoslavia during Operation Allied Force in early 1999. One is seen here landing at Aviano in April. (Key – Alan Warnes)

Below: While the rest of the world focused on operations over Yugoslavia, VFA-37 and other CVW-3 units were performing daily missions in support of Operation Southern Watch. Here, one of the unit's F/A-18Cs passes over USS *Enterprise* prior to recovery.(USN – Lt Jeff Cooper)

Middle: Two F/A-18Cs from VFA-22 the 'Fighting Redcocks' are seen here receiving fuel from a VC.10 K.3 from 101 Squadron, normally based at Royal Air Force, Brize Norton, Oxfordshire, UK.

US Navy F/A-18s also took part in the rescue of Major Scott O'Grady on June 2, 1995, although they only flew top cover during that mission. When a Serbian mortar attack on a crowded market in Sarajevo killed 37 people, NATO launched Operation Deliberate Force on August 30, 1995. Hornets from VMFA (AW)-533 at Aviano took part with F/A-18Cs from USS *Theodore Roosevelt* and Spanish EF-18s.

Operation Desert Fox began as a result of Saddam Hussein failing to comply with United Nations weapons inspection teams and forcing these teams out of Iraq. Hornets from VFA-37 VFA-105 and aircraft from VMFA-312 were assigned to USS *Enterprise* when the four days of attacks began on December 16, 1998. The three units flew missions carrying a range of ordnance, including 2,000lb (907kg) GBU-24 Precision Guided Munitions (PGM), together with the first operational use of AGM-154 JSOW. Several aircraft flew sorties, dropping ADM-

141 Tactical Air Launched Decoys (TALD) to foil Iraqi air defence systems.

Another first during Operation Desert Fox was the debut of female aircrew flying fast jets on combat operations, unlike previous wars when they had flown only in support aircraft. One of the female pilots was assigned to VFA-37 at the time. The next conflict involving Hornets began in the spring of 1999, when negotiations for a peaceful settlement to end Serbian ethnic cleansing failed and Slobodan Milosevic refused to withdraw his forces from Kosovo. Operation Allied Force began on March 24, 1999. F/A-18s were involved in the action from the start. They comprised six Spanish Hornets from Esc 121 of Ala 12, mainly carrying GBU-16s and operating from Aviano, alongside 21 Canadian CF-18s from four different units.

As the campaign continued, 24 USMC F/A-18Ds from VMFA (AW)-332 and -533 were deployed to Taszar in Hungary on May 23. They began operations on May 30. US Navy Hornets from VFA-15, and VFA-87 aboard USS *Theodore Roosevelt* performed both as fighters with AIM-9 and AIM-120 and as bombers launching AGM-154 JSOWs and AGM-65 Mavericks while they also undertook SEAD duties.

Following the terrorist atrocities at the World Trade Center and the Pentagon on September 11, 2001, the US Navy deployed USS *George Washington* and USS *John F Kennedy* off the US eastern seaboard to protect New York and Washington. Other Hornets from both active and reserve units began flying Combat Air Patrol missions around these and other cities, as well as major industrial sites. The US Government, which had evidence that the hijackers were involved with Usama bin Laden and his al-Qaeda terrorist organisation, requested that the Taliban regime in Afghanistan hand over bin Laden, who had been using the country as a base since 1996.

When the Taliban failed to comply, with the demand, Operation Enduring Freedom began on October 7, with F/A-18s in action from the start. Initial operations were undertaken by VFA-22, VFA-94 and VFA-97 aboard USS *Carl Vinson*, and VFA-151 VFA-192 and -195 from USS *Kitty Hawk*, both ships having diverted from normal operations in the Pacific. USS *Enterprise*, which was en route home from a cruise in the Indian Ocean, with VFA-15 and VFA-87 embarked, diverted to take part in the early stages of the campaign. USS *Theodore Roosevelt* sailed from the USA shortly after the terrorist attacks, with VFA-82, VFA-86 and VMFA-251 aboard, and formally relieved the *Enterprise* in mid-October.

USS *John C Stennis*, with VFA-146 and VFA-147 and VMFA-314 aboard, arrived on station in late November 2001 to replace the *Carl Vinson*. Australia joined the growing international coalition against the war on terrorism when they deployed four F/A-18s to Diego Garcia to perform air defence duties around the island in September, returning to the RAAF base at Williamtown at the end of May 2002.

US Navy F/A-18s took part in Operation Anaconda in early March to attack al-Qaeda and Taliban positions in mountains around the town of Zormat. The USMC deployed six F/A-18Ds from VMFA (AW)-121 to Manas air

Left: An F/A-18C from VFA-195 prepares to refuel from a USAF Boeing KC-135 from the 319th Air Expeditionary Group during Operation Enduring Freedom on October 26, 2001. (USAF – T/Sgt Scott Reed)

Right: The 'Mighty Shrikes' of VFA-94 was another unit aboard USS *Carl Vinson* as part of CVW-11, diverted from routine operations to participate in the opening phase of Operation Enduring Freedom. This F/A-18C is releasing flares during a training mission on October 31, 2001. (USN – Lt Steve Lightstone)

Right: With training missions over, the serious missions to Afghanistan began. The CAG bird of VFA-94 was captured shortly before refuelling from a USAF KC-135R on November 4, 2001. (USN – Lt Ken Koelbl)

Right: The squadron commander's aircraft and CAG bird from VMFA-251 wears full-colour squadron marking in common with most other commanders' aircraft within the Air Wing. (Key – Alan Warnes)

Right: A pair of Hornets waits on the catapults aboard USS *Roosevelt* in November 2001. The nearest aircraft belongs to the 'Thunderbolts' of VMFA-251 while the rear aircraft is from VFA-86 'Sidewinders'. (Key – Alan Warnes)

base in Kyrgyzstan in April 2002. These aircraft were equipped with the ATARS system and took part in subsequent bombing operations to clean up remaining pockets of opposition.

They were joined by more Hornets from units aboard USS *John F Kennedy,* which replaced the Roosevelt in March 2002. The first operational deployment of the F/A-18E Super Hornet was in July 2002, when VFA-115 began operations aboard USS *Abraham Lincoln.* The unit initially flew missions over Afghanistan, although it was never called upon to drop any weapons.

The Super Hornet's first combat mission was in early November, when Iraqi air defence forces opened fired on coalition aircraft over the Southern No-Fly Zone. In response to these attempts to shoot down coalition aircraft, attacks were launched on two SAM batteries at a site near Al Kut. An attack was also launched on the Command and Control Communications (C3i) facility near Tallil using JDAMs on November 6, and the unit went on to perform two further combat sorties.

In the early months of 2003, Western concerns began to deepen with regard to Saddam Hussein's failure to comply fully with numerous requests from the United Nations' weapons inspectors for greater co-operation in their search for Iraqi weapons of mass destruction (WMD). The most active critics of Saddam's policy were the United States and the United Kingdom, who desperately attempted to obtain a 'second' UN resolution to authorise the use of military action should the Iraqi régime fail to comply. (The 'first' resolution, 1441, provided no new authorisation for the use of force and is, indeed, only one of a series of UN resolutions arising out of Resolution 687, which defined the cease-fire terms at the end of the 'first' Gulf War).

Intense diplomatic efforts continued throughout February and into early March, thwarted by the French decision to use its veto in the UN Security Council whatever the outcome and exacerbated by German, Russian and Chinese unwillingness to support the call for a 'sec-

ond resolution'. As the threat of war loomed ever nearer, a large contingency deployment of US military forces was announced, including the dispatch of an eventual six US Navy aircraft carriers to the Gulf region.

Following the collapse of the UK-US diplomatic effort in mid-March to secure the vital 'second' UN resolution, Australia was one of the few countries willing to commit combat aircraft to action in support of US and British air assets. The Australian Prime Minister, John Howard, subsequently confirmed on March 18 that the squadron of Royal Australian Air Force (RAAF) Hornets, which had been deployed to the Gulf region as a contingency measure in early February, would participate alongside US and

Top: Ground crew prepare an F/A-18 from VFA-82 'Marauders' for launching from the *Theodore Roosevelt* in November 2001. (Key – Alan Warnes)

Above: An unusual task performed by F/A-18s during Operation Enduring Freedom took place on January 20, 2002, when a pair of Hornets bombed a Marine Corps' CH-53E that crashed in a remote location in Afghanistan. Having been deemed unsalvageable, it was decided that bombing would prevent parts from being pilfered from the wreckage. (Key – Dave Willis)

Left: The 'Wildcats' of VFA-136 were assigned to CVW-7 aboard USS *John F Kennedy* throughout early 2002. (USN – Lt Cmdr Christopher W Chope)

Left: Smoke pours from the main undercarriage tyres of this 'Dambusters' Hornet as it attempts to catch the arrestor wire aboard USS *Kitty Hawk* after performing a combat mission over Afghanistan. (USN – John E Woods)

British warplanes in planned air operations against the Iraqi régime. The 14 Hornets and their air and ground crews were drawn from No 75 Squadron RAAF based at Tindal near Darwin, the entire Australian contingent of air and ground forces operating under the auspices of Operation Falconer in support of the coalition effort. Operation Iraqi Freedom commenced on March 20, with the stated aim being to effect a 'régime change' by removing Saddam Hussein from power, dismantling the apparatus of State control vested in the ruling Ba'ath Party and to seek out and destroy Iraq's WMD stocks.

The 'Coalition of the Willing', some 48 member states of the UN, from Afghanistan to Uzbekistan, and including certain key Arab states, had also pledged to assist the Iraqi people with deliveries of food and medical supplies. After the initial strikes on Baghdad, using ship-launched Tomahawk cruise missiles, F/A-18 Hornet strike aircraft began offensive operations alongside other coalition combat aircraft. The parent carriers for the Hornets included the USS *Theodore Roosevelt* and the USS *Harry S Truman*, operating in the Mediterranean Sea, supported by the USS *Kitty Hawk*, the USS *Constellation* and USS *Abraham Lincoln* in the Persian Gulf. The USS *Nimitz* was initially held in reserve somewhere in the Pacific Ocean. The US Marine Corps deployed several of its squadrons to various land bases in the theatre of operations to support US

Right: A pilot from VFA-131 during a combat patrol over Afghanistan in early 2002. (USN)

Below: An ATARS-equipped F/A-18D from VMFA (AW)-121 taxying past a line of French Air Force Mirage 2000Ds at Manas air base in Kyrgyzstan. The squadron arrived on April 16, 2002, and while it was forward deployed, the unit notched up 4,846 flight hours without a single mishap before returning home at the beginning of October. (USAF – Master Sgt Jerry King)

Right: At the beginning of 2003, all six versions of the Hornet stood ready to perform combat missions at any time, anywhere around the world, day or night. (Key – Alan Warnes)

Marines and coalition ground forces. In addition to the units already aboard the carriers, VMFA-251 was deployed to Kuwait, while VMFA-232 operated from an undisclosed location.

Among the many missions carried out during the early stages of the conflict, one of the more notable events occurred on March 25, involving two F/A-18Cs from VFA-151 operating from the USS *Constellation*. The two aircraft were tasked against time-critical targets, one of which was believed to have been an Iraqi Navy gunboat in the vicinity of Umm Qasr. One Hornet independently identified and subsequently destroyed the first two targets. The second of the two Hornets then 'laser designated' the third target, reported to have been a gunboat. This enabled a Lockheed Martin S-3B Viking of VS-38 to launch an AGM-65E Maverick laser-guided missile at the target, which homed onto the vessel, guided by the reflected beam of the Hornet's laser designator. This is believed to have been the first live launch in combat of a Maverick missile by the Viking.

Australian F/A-18s initially performed escort duties for high-value assets (HVA) including tankers and airborne early warning aircraft, although they also commenced bombing operations towards the end of the first week of combat. This marked the first time that Australian Hornets had dropped bombs in a conflict and also marked the first time that No.75 Squadron RAAF had participated in combat operations since World War Two.

Above right: An unusual angle of an F/A-18A from VFA-97, captured on finals to land aboard the USS *Nimitz*, after conducting a training mission while participating in Operation Enduring Freedom during March 2003.
(USN - Airman Maebel Tinoko)

Right: VMFA-232 flew combat operations from the start of Operation Iraqi Freedom, here one of the unit's more colourful aircraft returns to its allocated mission after refuelling from a USAF KC-135 Stratotanker.
(USAF - S/Sgt Cherie A Thurlby)

Below: Maintenance crews from 75 Squadron Royal Australian Air Force prepare several F/A-18s for flight.
(Australian Department of Defence)

Left: Both the air wings assigned to the USS *Harry S Truman* and the USS *Theodore Roosevelt* on station in the Mediterranean performed operations. This VMFA-115 F/A-18A+ departs on another mission in March 2003. (USN - PMA Aaron Burden)

Centre: The US Navy reserve unit VFA-201 was called to active duty in November 2002 and undertook missions during Operation Iraqi Freedom while assigned to Carrier Air Wing Eight. (USN - PM1 Michael W Pendergrass)

Bottom: An F/A-18A+ from VMFA-115 taxies across the flight deck of the USS *Harry S Truman* during the early stages of Operation Iraqi Freedom. (USN - PM1 Michael W Pendergrass)

A BAE Sea Harrier FRS.1
pulls into a vertical loop
with a tiger-striped CF-
18A of No.439 Squadron
Canadian Forces in 1991.
(Joe Mercer – Royal Navy)